Nosferatu

An Opera Libretto

(Based on the Film by F. W. Murnau)

- B Y -

Dana Gioia

Graywolf Press

SAINT PAUL, MINNESOTA

Publication of this volume is made possible in part by a grant provided by the Minnesota State Arts Board through an appropriation by the Minnesota State Legislature, and by a grant from the National Endowment for the Arts. Significant support has also been provided by the Bush Foundation; Dayton's Project Imagine with support from Target Foundation; the McKnight Foundation; a grant made on behalf of the Stargazer Foundation; and other generous contributions from foundations, corporations, and individuals. To these organizations and individuals we offer our heartfelt thanks.

Funding for this volume has been graciously provided by John Ebey.

The author wishes to thank the many editors who have supported this project through its long development. Individual songs and arias from *Nosferatu* appeared in *Acumen, Evansville Review, The Formalist, River Styx,* and *Northeast Corridor,* which also published the vocal score of "Ellen's Dream." The original scenario for the opera appeared in the *Review.* The full libretto was serialized in three successive issues of *Sparrow,* which also published an early version of "*Sotto Voce.*" The final version of "*Sotto Voce*" appeared online in the *Woodbine.* Parts of the opera and libretto have also been broadcast on KPFA's *Cover to Cover* and BBC's *Night Waves.*

Published by Graywolf Press
2402 University Avenue, Suite 203
Saint Paul, Minnesota 55114
All rights reserved.

www.graywolfpress.org

Published in the United States of America

ISBN 1-55597-319-1

2 4 6 8 9 7 5 3 1
First Graywolf Printing, 2001

Library of Congress Catalog Number: 00-105079

Cover still from F. W. Murnau's *Nosferatu*

Cover design: Jeanne Lee

Nosferatu

Also by Dana Gioia

POETRY

Daily Horoscope
The Gods of Winter
Interrogations at Noon

CRITICAL COLLECTIONS

Can Poetry Matter?: Essays on Poetry and American Culture
The Barrier of a Common Language: Essays on Contemporary British Poetry

TRANSLATIONS

Mottetti: Poems of Love by Eugenio Montale
The Madness of Hercules by Seneca

EDITED BY DANA GIOIA

The Ceremony and Other Stories by Weldon Kees
Poems from Italy (with William Jay Smith)
New Italian Poets (with Michael Palma)
Certain Solitudes: Essays on the Poetry of Donald Justice (with William Logan)
An Introduction to Poetry (with X. J. Kennedy)
An Introduction to Fiction (with X. J. Kennedy)
Literature: An Introduction to Fiction, Poetry, and Drama (with X. J. Kennedy)
The Longman Anthology of Short Fiction (with R. S. Gwynn)

Contents

Foreword   ix
by Anne Williams

Nosferatu   3

**Sotto Voce: Notes
on the Libretto as a Literary Form**   67

Foreword

Listening to the Children of the Night:
The Vampire and Romantic Mythology

by

Anne Williams

Listen to them—the children of the night—
what music they make!

—Bram Stoker, *Dracula* (1897; Chapter 2)

I.

The first important vampire in English literature is less a vampire than a figure of speech. He appears in a melodramatic curse spoken by a character in Lord Byron's early poem, *The Giaour* (1813). Byron had recently returned to England from a Grand Tour that included Greece, Turkey, and Albania in addition to the more conventional capitals of western Europe. He brought back a picturesque Albanian costume that he wore to costume balls and a store of information about those distant and exotic lands. "If I am a poet," he told his friend Edward Trelawny, "the air of Greece has made me one." Byron began publishing verse romances at the rate of two a year. These included the spectacularly best-selling *Childe Harold I* and *II* (1812) and the so-called "oriental" or "eastern" tales. Besides *The Giaour,* he wrote *The Bride of Abydos* (1813), *The Corsair* and *Lara* (1814), and *Parisina* and *The Siege of Corinth* (1816). These poems offered his adoring public pleasures nowadays promised by summer blockbuster movies: sex and violence in an exotic location. "I awoke to find myself famous," he duly noted in his journal.

To give his tales an authentic flavor, Byron sprinkled them with words likely to be unfamiliar to his audience, which he helpfully annotated. "Vampire," like "Rahmadan" (as he spelled it) and "Giaour" itself, was one of these:

> The Vampire superstition is still general in the Levant. Honest Tournefort tells a long story, which Mr. Southey, in the notes on Thalaba quotes about those 'Vroucolochas', as he calls them. The Romaic term is 'Vardoulacha.' I recollect a whole family being terrified by the scream of a child, which they imagined must proceed from such a visitation. The Greeks never mention the word without horror. I find that 'Broucolokas' is an old legitimate

Hellenic appellation—at least is so applied to Arsenius, who, according to the Greeks, was after his death animated by the Devil—the moderns, however, use the word I mention.

Anchoring the most improbable narratives in a semblance of reality is a time-honored technique for the writer of romantic, and especially horror, fiction. Even Coleridge, more than a decade after publishing "The Rime of the Ancient Mariner," decided to add marginal glosses to his poem, a mode of annotation that already seemed a bit old-fashioned to an early nineteenth-century audience. But the notes' archaic language and learned if sometimes irrelevant comments implied that a thorough if unimaginative scholar had taken this peculiar and puzzling tale seriously. Hence they lend a certain authenticity to the Mariner's fantastic voyage. Juxtaposing the learned discourse with the improbable tale offers the reader a certain reassurance that there *is* a rational explanation for all this. Psychologically, the technique of mixing the seemingly factual with the completely implausible creates a Freudian "compromise formation": on the one hand, the fantasy seems anchored in the real world, often by a supposed eyewitness account. On the other, the more rational commentary also frames the tale as genuinely "other," as something weird and desperately in need of explanation, encouraging the reader to suspend his disbelief that *anything* could happen in a place so remote from ours.

The Giaour created a sensation. Even the ironic Jane Austen was apparently one of its attentive readers. In *Persuasion* (1818), the heroine Anne Elliot and her acquaintance, the bookish and melancholy Captain Harville, discuss how Byron's title word, which means "infidel," should be pronounced. (The "g" is soft, thus *jowr*.) Although the O. E. D. records the use of the word "vampire" in a traveler's account as early as 1734, one may safely assume that it became widely familiar to a moderately well-educated audience only after 1813.

Here is the curse Byron composed:

> But first, on earth as Vampire sent,
> Thy corse shall from its tomb be rent;
> Then ghastly haunt thy native place,
> And suck the blood of all thy race,
> There from thy daughter, sister, wife,
> At midnight drain the stream of life;
> Yet loathe the banquet which perforce
> Must feed thy livid living corse;

Thy victims ere they yet expire
Shall know the daemon as their sire
As cursing thee, thou cursing them,
Thy flowers are withered on the stem.

The object of this ghastly curse is Byron's hero, the Giaour himself. A Christian living in a Muslim country, he has fallen in love with Leila, one of the sultan's harem. Somehow the two manage to consummate this relationship, though the reader never learns how. As the Giaour evasively says, "I lov'd her— love will find its way / Through paths where wolves would fear to prey." When the affair is discovered, Leila suffers the cruel punishment here accorded unfaithful wives: she is sewn into a sack and thrown into the sea. The Giaour avenges her death by killing her murderer. He returns to Europe, where he chooses to become another kind of infidel, an atheist who retreats into a monastery, eventually half-divulging his history and his enduring passion for his lost Leila as he dies.

In these early works Byron was perfecting a new archetype, the Byronic hero, or *homme fatal*. Like Milton's Satan, who first appears in *Paradise Lost* (1671) as an "archangel ruin'd," this character is thoroughly paradoxical. He is a man of action, yet also capable of intense passion and feminine sensitivity. Milton's Satan was tortured by remorse for the rebel angels who had followed him into battle with God and then into Hell, but Byron's Giaours and Conrads and Laras are tortured by romantic love. The object of their passion is always the unattainable woman they are fated to destroy. And their passion is equal to Satan's infernal "fiery deluge fed / With ever-burning sulphur unconsumed"; as the Giaour exclaims, "The cold of clime are cold of blood / Their love can scarce deserve the name / But mine was like the lava flood / That boils in Aetna's breast of flame."

The Byronic hero is not exactly handsome, but he is magnetically attractive, with a piercing gaze and an air of mystery. His face seems to signify that he is haunted by the memory of some terrible crime. Like Satan, the Byronic hero is an outsider and an overreacher, though the divine Law that he violates is not the First Commandment but the Seventh, a sin often involving not only adultery but incest. This genealogy of the Byronic hero should not be surprising, since the poets that we now call "Romantic" considered Milton's Satan a more interesting and dramatic character than his God. Attempting to account for the poet's success with his fallen angel in *Paradise Lost*, Blake declared (in *The*

Marriage of Heaven and Hell, 1790–93) that "Milton was a true poet and of the devil's party without knowing it." In fact, Byron and Shelley's reviewers described them not as "Romantics," but as members of "the Satanic School."

Thus the vampire enters English literature in the distinguished company of a Byronic hero: indeed, as his dark double. The curse quoted above shows that the vampire is also always doomed to kill the thing he loves. If Byronic heroes sometimes transgress that most "natural" of laws, the incest taboo, the vampire merely enacts a more material version of a similarly "unnatural" compulsion: not the consummation of a forbidden love, but the consumption of the beloved's blood. Yet the vampire's relation to Byron and the Byronic hero is even more complicated. In the summer of 1816 Byron left England forever, following his own possible violation of the incest taboo. His wife, Annabella, Lady Byron, had filed for divorce after only one year of marriage. It was widely rumored that she had discovered an affair between Byron and his half-sister Augusta Leigh. We cannot be sure whether these rumors were true, but Byron left England and he was not loath to exploit the scandal in the following months, as he composed *Childe Harold III* (in which Byron/Harold sends a love lyric to his sister), and *Manfred,* a closet drama about a Faustian character haunted by the death of *his* sister Astarte.

II.

And so, one year after the Battle of Waterloo, Byron traveled across Europe, accompanied by his personal physician Dr. John Polidori. They settled at the Villa Diodati on the shores of Lake Geneva. He was joined there soon afterwards by Percy Bysshe Shelley, his wife Mary Godwin Shelley, and her stepsister Clare Clairmont, who had, like many another starstruck young woman of Regency England, pursued and seduced the glamorous Lord Byron. During the month of July 1816, the weather near Geneva was cold and rainy. The company amused themselves by reading Gothic novels and Coleridge's poem "Christabel," which had been composed in 1797 but only recently published. It concerns a young woman, Christabel, who one April midnight goes into the woods outside her father's castle, "to pray / For the weal of her lover that's far away." There beneath a "huge broad-breasted old oak tree," she discerns, by the light of the full moon, a strange sight: a beautiful, barefooted woman dressed in white silk and glittering with jewels. She tells Christabel that her name is Geraldine and that she has been abducted by five "warriors" and then abandoned. The compassionate Christabel invites her back to the castle. But at the threshold Geraldine suddenly grows weak, and her hostess has to carry her over the threshold. When they reach Christabel's chamber, Geraldine undresses, exposing a bosom horribly disfigured in some undisclosed way. She lies down beside Christabel and takes her in her arms. First bidding the girl's guardian spirit, the ghost of her mother, to depart ("This hour is mine!") Geraldine casts a spell ensuring that although Christabel will remember what happened this night, she will not be able to tell anyone.

The following morning Geraldine awakens full of energy, while Christabel is curiously languid. Her widowed father Sir Leoline is much taken with his unexpected and beautiful guest, and Christabel is incapable of telling him what she knows about her, being reduced to a snake-like hissing. The resident Bard recounts his dream of the previous night, a vision of Sir Leoline's white dove (also named Christabel) being strangled by a bright green snake. Sir Leoline quickly interprets the dream as concerning the abducted Geraldine, whom he believes to be the daughter of a long-lost friend of his youth. There the poem breaks off. For the rest of his life Coleridge declared his intention to finish it, but he never did. Even as a fragment—or perhaps *because* it is one— "Christabel" is powerful poetry.

Having exhausted the entertainments of Coleridge's poem and the handful of Gothic novels with which the company was furnished, Byron proposed that they each should write a ghost story. And so all of them set to work. Mary conceived *Frankenstein,* which would be published in 1818. The other work to emerge from the contest was the first vampire novel in English, Polidori's *The Vampyre.* Byron had began a novel about a vampire traveling in modern Greece who before "dying" and undergoing a mock burial, elicits an oath from his human traveling companion that he will say nothing of what he has seen. Returning to London sometime later, the companion finds the vampire very much alive, and preying on young women. Bound by his oath, however, he can say nothing, even though his own sister becomes the vampire's final victim.

Byron wrote the first chapter, which describes the oath and the "death." But he had, it seems, outlined the rest of it in some detail, and apparently Polidori took careful notes of his employer's intentions. He completed the novel on his own and in 1819 published *The Vampyre,* with an introductory note describing events at the villa during the summer of 1816 and attributing the novel to Byron. He could have done nothing better calculated to achieve widespread interest in this slim book. Confident that they were reading a novel by Byron, the public responded enthusiastically. Polidori then confessed the truth, insisting that although the "ground work" was Byron's, the novel was in fact his own. When a second edition appeared, the publisher continued to declare that it was Byron's, knowing good publicity when he saw it.

Stories, especially the ones we want to hear again and again, inevitably reflect the fears and desires of those who tell them. As long as men told most of our stories, fatal women were everywhere, from Medusa and Eve through Keats's "La Belle Dame sans Merci" (1819). (This is not to say that women were entirely silent: Chaucer's garrulous Wife of Bath immediately comes to mind, though she is, of course, a man's creation.) Thus the rather sudden appearance of the fatal *man,* the Byronic hero and his vampire shadow, during the literary Romantic period (roughly 1780–1830), implies, among other things, a profound if unconscious shift in post-Enlightenment cultural assumptions about gender, the erosion of millennia of a patriarchal culture and its fundamental misogyny.

The Byronic hero reflects one of British Romanticism's most startling innovations: the importation, into high culture, of things traditionally regarded as "feminine" and therefore unimportant, such as nature, emotions, imagination, children. As we have seen the Byronic hero is divided between a "masculine," conquering self, and a "feminine," suffering one. No doubt one reason for Byron's huge success with his female readers was his ability to show himself a feeling as much as a thinking being and a victim of forces beyond his control. What Byron called "fate" his female readers experienced as the constraints of a culture that offered women little power of any kind. What is novel, and what would be revolutionary, about the Byronic hero, therefore, is that he is a man who enjoys the privileges of the aristocratic and powerful, but he also experiences the world from a subordinate, "feminine" perspective. To be obliged to feel as well as to think is to be cursed, as any nineteenth-century British aristocrat would have felt if he had suddenly been compelled to live life as a woman.

The Romantics were undoubtedly unconscious of the deeper cultural implications of what their literary revolution implied about gender and patriarchal social arrangements. Presumably it never occurred to Wordsworth that in elevating intuition, imagination, and the child he was giving new power to the culturally "feminine." (Although during his lifetime the civil and political status of women was widely debated in public for the first time ever.) The sense that threatening changes were in progress was signified in the same way that the unconscious expresses its fears in nightmares. "Myths are public dreams," wrote Jung. Throughout the nineteenth century, the vampire was one such symbol expressing anxiety about rising female power and widespread cultural change.

III.

For the rest of the century vampires proliferated in popular culture. They appear as male and female, young and old, foreign and domestic. In the decades following the waning of Romanticism in the 1830s, the vampire because a stock figure of pulp fiction, most of it now forgotten. Specialists in the Gothic tradition still remember, and occasionally read, *Varney the Vampire,* a long-running serial publication, a kind of soap opera with a vampire, an unlikely predecessor of *Dark Shadows,* perhaps. But Sheridan Le Fanu's novella, "Carmilla" (1872), is the most significant of the Victorian vampire tales, for it links Romantic vampires and their late-Victorian "grandchild," Dracula. Like "Christabel," which Le Fanu obviously knew, "Carmilla" concerns the introduction of a female vampire into the household of a widowed father and his motherless daughter Laura.

Bram Stoker knew Le Fanu's story. "Christabel" and "Carmilla" had established a number of conventions that he would use: that vampires must be invited into the house by a member of the family, that they may be bound by certain seemingly arbitrary conditions, such as the letters of a name or the need to have a coffin as a home base. Le Fanu also popularized the stake through the heart as a means of dispatching the vampire. Most interesting and important, however, is the idea implied in Coleridge and made explicit in "Carmilla," that vampire and victim feel an erotic attraction for each other. Lord Ruthven, Byronic hero that he is, is a lady-killer who attacks marriageable women, and actually marries one of them, but Polidori does not suggest that they felt a sexual attraction for him. There is more emphasis on the charm of his wealth and aristocratic lineage.

Dracula (1897), however, created the vampire myth as we know it: that vampires fear garlic and the cross; that vampires sleep in their coffins of native earth; that they are associated with bats and wolves; that the vampire's victim becomes a vampire; that they are the "Un-dead"—*Nosferatu.* Stoker's working title for his novel was "The Un-dead." In the course of his research, however (and he did a great deal of it), he found a much better one. He decided to align his vampire with a historical personage, the Transylvanian tyrant, Vlad the Impaler, sometimes called *Dracul* (dragon). This was a brilliant choice. Seeing his vampire as the monster that threatens Western culture itself, he created a myth that has haunted our collective imagination for a century.

In Stoker's version, Dracula is an aristocrat from barbarous, mysterious Transylvania. (He thus comes from "through the woods.") The last of an ancient family, he moves to London in search of new blood. He preys first on Lucy Westenra, a pretty, flirtatious, but unstable young woman given to sleepwalking, who receives three proposals of marriage in one day and wonders aloud to her friend Mina Murray Harker why she can't accept them all. Lucy has a formidable array of allies in her three would-be husbands: Arthur, Lord Godalming, Dr. John Seward, and the Texan Quincey Morris; plus Mina's husband Jonathan Harker, and Dr. Van Helsing. The Dutch Van Helsing is Dr. Seward's mentor, and both a physician and an expert on the occult. Despite their best efforts, Lucy dies and becomes a vampire. At Van Helsing's insistence, the men open Lucy's coffin and drive a stake through her heart, thus ensuring that she be truly dead. (The "honor" of driving the stake is accorded Arthur, who would have been her husband.) Meanwhile, Dracula turns his attentions to Mina, who is more strong-minded than Lucy. (According to Van Helsing, she has "a man's brain and a woman's heart.") Aware of what is happening to her, she struggles to aid the men in their conquest of Dracula by exploiting the telepathic connection she now has with her predator. Eventually they follow him back to Castle Dracula and kill him, though Quincey also dies in the struggle. Mina, now safe, gives birth to a son named for all five of Dracula's conquerors.

This last and most influential version of the nineteenth-century vampire myth records a backlash against the Romantics' revolutionary embrace of the culturally feminine. In "Christabel" and "Carmilla," both significant precursors of *Dracula,* the vampire is a woman who preys on women. The notion of a same-sex vampire attack raises the specter of same-sex eroticism, which was by the end of the century increasingly pathologized by writers such as Freud, Kraft-Ebbing, and Havelock Ellis; Stoker may have shrunk from such implications. *Dracula* does have female vampires, but they are subordinate—the brides in his castle and poor Lucy, whose vampire career is very short—and all of them are satisfied to feed on infants. Stoker in fact wrote an episode concerning a female vampire who preys on Jonathan Harker, but he eventually published it instead as a short story, "Dracula's Guest." In *Dracula,* vampires are heterosexual and thoroughly demonized. Although Stoker mentions his villain's tragic circumstances as the last of his kind, he aligns his creation less with his "father," Lord Byron than with his "grandfather," Milton's Satan.

Stoker also casts his vampire tale as a cultural struggle between the new, bourgeois, scientific, progressive, and enlightened West and the old, superstitious, dark, and dangerous East. Among other things, Count Dracula is a decadent aristocrat. But Van Helsing and his crew specifically struggle with the demon for—what else?—control of the women.

IV.

Given the melodramatic power of vampires to fascinate and move the reader, it is surprising that—until Dana Gioia and Alva Henderson—the vampire has almost never excited the imagination of the opera librettist or composer. Byron's oriental tale, which gave birth to the creature, is certainly "operatic" in theme and technique: until he began composing *Don Juan,* the last work of his career, his works were, like much nineteenth-century opera, excessive, fatal, and tragic. His earlier poetry inspired an extraordinary number of orchestral composers including Berlioz and Tchaikovsky; Donizetti composed an opera based on *Parisina* (1833), and Verdi wrote two, *I due Foscari* (1844) and *Il Corsaro* (1848). *Grove* lists forty more operas based on Byron, mostly by forgotten composers. In the nineteenth century, there is one exception to the no-vampire rule: Heinrich Marschner's *Der Vampyr* (1828). As a young man of twenty, Marschner (1795–1861) gained an audience with Beethoven, who reportedly commented after looking at his music, "Don't come too often." Wagner, on the other hand, admired him and quotes one of his themes in *Die Walküre.* First performed in Leipzig with considerable success, the libretto of *Der Vampyr* was written by Marschner's brother-in-law, Wilhelm August Wohlbrük, and is based on Polidori's novel, though with some significant changes. Here Lord Ruthven's final victim is not Aubrey's sister, but Malwina, the woman with whom he is secretly in love. Instead of being doomed to watch Ruthven kill her because he is bound to keep his oath, in this version Aubrey reveals that this man is a vampire. Ruthven is struck by lightning and burns to death. Aubrey and Malwina are married. Though rare, *Der Vampyr* is still occasionally performed.

The paucity of vampire operas in the nineteenth century must be related to the larger question of why the Gothic tradition (to which the vampire belongs) itself inspired so few operas, at least operas that have survived in the repertoire. Donizetti's *Lucia di Lammermoor,* based on a novel by Sir Walter Scott, is the only unambiguously canonical opera with strong affinities to literary Gothic.

(The haunted heroine is subjected to violence in the bosom of her family and goes mad in order to escape it.) Yet Herbert Lindenberger remarks on the aesthetic similarities between opera and the Gothic in *Opera: The Extravagant Art* (1984): "It is the one form of fiction that pursued the high style systematically in the last two centuries. . . . Like opera the Gothic was a popular form whose public recognized its artifice and its distance from ordinary life on the one hand and on the other, its power and immediacy of effect."

It may be that Gothic works were already so "operatic" in effect that they didn't seem to cry out for that passionate heightening in which opera specializes. It may be that since the Gothic flourished most impressively in English, which at that time lacked a native operatic tradition, English Gothic works were less likely to catch the attention of continental librettists, although the plethora of operas based on Sir Walter Scott's novels weakens that hypothesis. Oddly, however, it is easy to think of arguably Gothic twentieth-century operas: Bartók's *Bluebeard's Castle,* Britten's *Turn of the Screw,* Goldschmidt's *Beatrice Cenci,* settings of *Wuthering Heights* by Carlisle Floyd and Bernard Herrmann, Argento's *Miss Havisham's Fire* and *The Voyage of Edgar Allan Poe,* Janáček's *Makropulos Affair,* Libby Larsen's *Frankenstein, or, the Modern Prometheus,* Moran's *Dracula Diary.* Of these, three (Bartók, Britten, and Janáček) are close to being standard repertoire, if not quite warhorses, but it remains to be seen whether the others will continue to be performed. Gothic tales have also seen quite spectacular successes on the twentieth-century Broadway stage, notably Sondheim's *Sweeney Todd,* and Lloyd Webber's *Phantom of the Opera.*

In an article published in the *Cambridge Opera Journal* (July 1999), Michael Grover-Friedlander considers "film's attraction to opera," which was there from the beginning. In 1910 Thomas Edison wrote, "We'll be ready for the moving picture show in a couple of months, but I'm not satisfied with that. I want to give grand opera." Grover-Freidlander argues that "operatic singing does not derive its force simply from the extravagance of the singing voice, but rather from its pointing to the limits of vocal expression and to meaninglessness." He continues, "Surprisingly, then, silent film is uniquely suited to go beyond song, in its fascination with and anxiety about, silence." In this essay Grover-Friedlander uses the 1925 silent film, *The Phantom of the Opera,* to explore this thesis, but the affinities he sees between the two forms are illuminating in the light of Dana Gioia's libretto *Nosferatu.*

Gioia liberates the vampire from the shadow of *Dracula* through the medium of a silent film, F. W. Murnau's *Nosferatu* (1922). Because of copyright restrictions, Murnau was forced to change Stoker's title and to change the story considerably. He moves it to Germany and collapses Mina and Lucy into one— Nina, a married woman in delicate health who shares Lucy's propensity to walk in her sleep. In Murnau's film, the vampire-hunters are eliminated and Dr. Van Helsing becomes an ineffectual local physician under a different name. Nina's husband, the Jonathan Harker character, succumbs to Nosferatu during his visit to Transylvania, and is thus of no help to her. Nosferatu, on the other hand, feels a predestined, fatal attraction to Nina and comes to find her. The rules of vampire destruction are changed as well. Here, to kill a vampire a woman must deceive him into remaining with her until after dawn, at which time the daylight will destroy him. This Nina accomplishes, at the cost of her own life.

As Gioia writes in his essay "Sotto Voce," "*Nosferatu* offered a librettist the positive virtues of a compelling plot, strong characters, and vivid, indeed often unforgettable, images." From the viewpoint of the literary critic, they also offered him the opportunity to return the myth of the vampire to its Byronic roots. Gioia's Nosferatu, Count Orlock, while echoing Dracula, also echoes the sentiments of Byron's Lara or Giaour: "I am the last survivor of my house, / You cannot understand how heavily the past / Weighs down on me.... How ancient deeds imprison us forever" (I, 3). As in the world of the Byronic hero, love is both fated and doomed. Upon seeing Ellen's portrait, he knows that she is his bride, and pursues her to the death. Like the Byronic hero, he is fundamentally paradoxical:

> I am the past that feeds upon the present.
> I am the darkness that daylight denies.
> I am the sins that you must inherit—
> The final truth in a world full of lies.
> I am the name that cannot be said.
> I am eternal, unliving, undead.
>
> (I, 3)

Or this:

> I am the darkness that falls from the sky,
> The blackness that brings you light,
> He who reveals your one true form—
> Cold, eternal, and bright.
>
> (II, 3)

In calling himself "The blackness that brings you light," Nosferatu aligns himself with his ancestor, Milton's Satan, whose name was Lucifer, "light-bringer."

But re-imagining the vampire myth as an opera has another important effect. For the first time in its evolution, at least through *Dracula*, the heroine/victim is not a merely a pawn in a contest between male adversaries. She is a heroine in her own right, as it were; she is the one who chooses and acts to destroy the vampire, although her choices are admittedly limited. One of the reasons she can do this, however, is that she is an operatic soprano; as with Lucia, she has a voice of her own. But she triumphs at the price of joining Nosferatu in death, in a dark but unmistakable *Liebestod*. It is, however, a love-death reminiscent less of *Tristan und Isolde* than of Senta and her beloved, another Byronic overreacher, Wagner's Flying Dutchman. Dana Gioia's *Nosferatu* is thus not only a libretto with strong ties to the traditions of Romantic opera, it also reveals the vampire's essential being as a Romantic archetype.

Anne Williams

Nosferatu

An Opera Libretto

for
Alva Henderson
prima la musica

Characters

ELLEN HUTTER, *a young woman*	*Soprano*
ERIC HUTTER, *her husband*	*Tenor*
COUNT ORLOCK, *later called* NOSFERATU, *a Hungarian nobleman*	*Bass Baritone*
HEINRICH SKULLER, *a businessman*	*Bass*
MARTHE LINK, *Ellen's sister*	*Mezzo-Soprano*
DR. FRANZ HARDING, *a specialist in nervous diseases*	*Baritone*
SERVANTS	
MONKS	
TOWNSPEOPLE	
MADMEN	
ASYLUM GUARDS	

Setting

The action of the opera takes place mostly in the Baltic seaport of Wisborg in the mid-nineteenth century.

Act One

The Counting House

The office of Heinrich Skuller. Whatever details of the setting are presented should suggest a busy, prosperous, but madly cluttered atmosphere. Skuller is a richly dressed but unkempt man in his sixties. His exaggerated attire and behavior reflect the eccentricity of a person whose ambitions exceed the small successes the town of Wisborg offers. As the scene opens, he sits working at a desk covered with ledgers. He takes an oversized letter on parchment out of an extravagant envelope bearing an immense red seal. He has read the letter before. Even though he sits at this desk, he exudes an almost unbearable level of nervous excitement. After a moment, he sees Eric Hutter, a man in his late twenties, arrive at the door.

SKULLER
Eric, come in! I'm glad you're here.
You've asked me many times about employment,
And I have said that I had nothing free.
But now, my friend, I have a proposition.

ERIC
A proposition? You have work for me?
How wonderful! My wife will be delighted.

SKULLER
Your new bride will have reason to be happy.
A bright young man like you deserves a chance.
You have responsibilities. Your wife—
So beautiful, so delicate, so weak.

5

You must look after her, and that takes money.
I have a proposition.

ERIC
What is it, sir?

SKULLER

He picks up the parchment letter but does not read from it. He holds it only as if to verify his statements.

A wealthy nobleman in Hungary—
Count Orlock is his name—has written me.
He wants to buy some property in town,
A large old house that he can renovate.
He needs to get away and find new life.
Life is so deadly dull in Hungary.

I've bought a place for him on speculation.
I've put my capital at risk. But if
We sell the house to him, there will be profit!

ERIC
You've bought some property in town? But where?

SKULLER
The empty manor house on Lindenplatz.

ERIC
Across the square from me? But it's a ruin!

SKULLER
What will he care? He wants to renovate.
And I want *you* to sell him the estate.
The Count is eager to do business.

ERIC
But it's a ruin. No one would buy that crypt.

SKULLER

But if you go to Hungary at once,
I think that we can sell it, sight unseen.
The Count is eager to do business.

Here is my proposition. Leave at once,
Sell him the house, and you keep half the profit.
The Count is eager to do business.

ERIC

But it's a ruin.

SKULLER

Repairs are easily made.

ERIC

You'll renovate?

SKULLER

And give you half the profit.

ERIC

He doesn't care?

SKULLER

You'll earn five thousand marks.

ERIC

I need to think this over.

SKULLER

Five thousand marks.

SKULLER

But is it right?

SKULLER

You must think of your wife . . .

ERIC

(*softly, as if it were a question*)

Ellen.

SKULLER

. . . so beautiful, so delicate.

ERIC

Ellen.

SKULLER

. . . so frail. She has no one but you.

ERIC

Five thousand marks?

SKULLER

A man must think of others.

ERIC

But she will worry if I go away.

SKULLER

He takes out a bottle of brandy and pours Eric a drink with an exaggerated show of cordiality.

A few weeks' pain will bring her years of ease.
This is your chance. I am too old to travel.
I need a bright young man to be my agent.
Will it be you? Or should I find another?
I can't delay. What if the Count looks elsewhere?

He leans toward Eric and whispers with grotesque intimacy.

I want to ask you something personal.
Do you know what you truly want from life?
Most people don't. That's why they seem half dead.

Remember happiness comes from embracing
Our true desires—whatever they may be.
You seem, my friend, at war within yourself—
Ambitious and yet strangely paralyzed.

ERIC

You'd laugh at me if I confessed my dreams.

SKULLER

Why would I ridicule a young man's hope?
Trust me. I want to help. No dream's too grand.

ERIC

My life has been a struggle from the first.
My father died when I was still a boy.
My youth has been all study, work, and waiting.

SKULLER

We have so much in common. Suffering,
Toil, and denial have been my life as well.
I want to help, but you must trust me first,
So tell me, Eric, tell me what you long for.

Aria: Eric's Confession

ERIC

What do I want?
I ache with desire.
I twist in its thorns.
I burn in its fire.
I hunger. I thirst.
But all that I want
Are the ordinary things
That every day brings
To anyone else.
I don't crave money

Or power or fame.
I only long
To be at ease
In my own life—
To wake at night
And never feel
The future pressing,
To eat a meal
And not taste fear,
To take delight
In what I learn,
In what I own,
In what I earn.
To feel my love
Deserves return.

But I am still a starving child
Standing in the dark,
Staring through a window
At a feast I cannot taste,
Watching the bright faces
Blessed with affection
I cannot share.
What do I desire?
A place at the table,
The warmth of the fire,
A circle of faces
Returning my smile—
To make a home
Worthy of my wife,
To forget the fears
That leave me driven
And deserve the love
I have been given.

SKULLER
You are a young man of feelings and ideals!
Laugh at you? Never! I applaud your strength.

Join me. You have a future in my firm.
I have no children. Help me in my work.
Why do you hesitate, my friend? Be practical.
Think of your wife. Is she provided for?

ERIC

We have no money, sir, but we are young.

Aria: Skuller's Advice

SKULLER

Never imagine the world will provide
Shoes for your children or a bed for your bride,
Bread for the table, a roof from the rain.
Turn away troubles, and they come again.
Whatever you love is easily lost.
A man must be strong whatever the cost.

It's easy to love like a softhearted youth
Lisping sweet lies to sugar the truth.
But what will you do when the times turn mean,
Your wife wears rags and your children grow lean?
Provide for your love or your love will be lost.
A man must be strong whatever the cost.

Duet Finale: The Agreement

SKULLER

Do you love your wife enough to make
Difficult choices for her sake?

ERIC

Yes, I love Ellen. I'd undertake
Any sort of labor for her sake.
But facing this journey, I feel lost.

SKULLER

A man must be strong whatever the cost!

ERIC

It's not about money, you understand.

SKULLER

But fear of a future we haven't planned.

ERIC

I don't crave money.

SKULLER

But don't despise
The safety and freedom that money buys.
Unless you provide, she may be lost.

ERIC

A man must be strong whatever the cost.

SKULLER	ERIC
You have no father. I have no son	I have no father. You have no son
To help me do what must be done.	To help you do what must be done.
Become my partner.	I'll be your partner.
Together we'll make	Together we'll make
Profit from all we undertake.	Profit from all we undertake.

TOGETHER

Provide for love or love will be lost.
A man must be strong whatever the cost.

SKULLER

Now, my young friend, your future is assured.

Skuller embraces him triumphantly. Stage fades to black.

The Dream

The parlor of the Hutters' apartment on Lindenplatz. The room is small and meagerly furnished but not untidy or uncomfortable. There are two doors: one leads to the outer hallway, the other to Ellen's bedroom. As the scene opens, Dr. Franz Harding, a prosperous physician in late middle age, sits taking notes. He is a cordial, learned man who has seen much of the world but little of it deeply. Marthe Link, Ellen's older sister, enters from the bedroom. Softly closing the door, Marthe signals the doctor to speak quietly. She crosses to his side. They confer.

HARDING

Is she still sleeping?

MARTHE

Yes, thank God, she is.

HARDING

(still adding to his notes)

How often does your sister have these spells—
The vivid dreams, the sleepwalking, the fevers?

MARTHE

Ellen has had these spells since we were young—
But never often, never so extreme.
When we were girls, I sometimes woke at night
To see her standing at the bedroom window
Staring for hours at the moonlit clouds.
Her eyes were open, but she was asleep.
I used to think that she could tell the future.
Is Ellen ill?

13

HARDING

Not ill and yet not well.
She isn't mad, if that's what worries you.
Not Ellen. No, if anything she is
Unnaturally lucid.
Her senses are amazingly acute.
She hears, sees, feels, even tastes everything
More vividly than other people do.
And she remembers everything as well.
She can relive a moment merely by
Recalling it. Even her dreams stay with her.
Is this a gift or curse? Imagine if
You lived in an eternal present tense,
The weight of all the past pressed down on you—
Incessant, tangible, exact, unchanging.
Her nerves are overwrought, as tightly stretched
As a stringed instrument that's tuned too high.
Played carefully, the sound is bright and clear,
But if it's roughly played, the strings will break.

MARTHE

When we were young, her dreams were wonderful,
But now they take such terrifying shapes.
Some nights she is afraid to fall asleep.
She dreams of hellish things—of catacombs
And plagues, of swarming rats, and worst of all,
Of being buried while she's still alive!

HARDING

Buried alive? She's buried every day
Beneath the unpaid bills, expenses, worry.
Her husband has no work. He barely has
Money enough to feed the two of them.
Such difficulties naturally embarrass
A sensitive young woman. Shame is powerful.
Her dreams are merely symbols that her mind
Produces to disguise anxiety—

She hides her real fears even from herself.
Ellen is delicate, but all she needs
Is rest—and some employment for her husband.

MARTHE

Thank you for treating her. We're in your debt.

HARDING

She interests me. I've never seen a case
Resembling hers. I'm working on a book
About somnambulism.

MARTHE

About what?

HARDING

Somnambulism—what you call sleepwalking,
A halfway state between a dream and trance.
I plan to push aside the superstition
And shine the light of science on the subject.

The door opens suddenly. Eric enters. He is conspicuously excited, even giddy, with the news of his employment. His entrance is so exuberant that Marthe quickly signals him to be quiet.

ERIC

Ellen! Where's Ellen?

MARTHE

Eric, please be quiet!

Ellen is sleeping!

ERIC

I have news for her.

MARTHE

Not now. She isn't well. The doctor's here.

ERIC

Yes, yes, I see. But I have news for her.
My news will do her good.

MARTHE
What is it, Eric?

ERIC

I have employment! And not just a job—
A future!

MARTHE
Bravo, Eric! Wonderful!

ERIC

I'm working for Herr Skuller. There is a chance
I could become a partner in his firm.

MARTHE
Wonderful. Wonderful.

HARDING
Yes, wonderful.
Just what the doctor ordered, don't you think?
This news will do more good for Ellen's health
Than all my medicine.

ERIC
I'm so excited.
This job is everything we ever hoped for.
I leave tomorrow for a business trip!

MARTHE
You leave? Tomorrow? Eric, how can you
Abandon Ellen in her present state?
She needs you with her. Doctor, talk to him.

HARDING
I think you should . . .

ERIC

I can't postpone this trip!

My chances at the firm depend on it.

HARDING

Perhaps you could . . .

MARTHE

You cannot think of leaving!

HARDING

I recommend . . .

ERIC

I must go! I have no choice!

HARDING

Stop arguing! We don't want to wake Ellen.

I think that Eric should feel free to leave.

Ellen is in no danger. You are here.

And I will stop by every afternoon.

The most important thing for her recovery

Is her security. This job's good news.

Men often must leave home to make a living.

Ellen suddenly enters from her bedroom. She stands for a moment at the door. Her hair is loose and disordered. She is dressed in an open white robe that does not hide her long, white nightgown. She has the intense but disoriented appearance of someone startled from sleep who does not yet entirely comprehend her surroundings. She seems oblivious to Marthe and Dr. Harding.

ELLEN

Eric, Eric, is it you?

Eric, Eric, you are here.

You woke me from a dream.

Eric starts to tell his news, but she silences him with a gesture.

Aria: Ellen's Dream

I came to a table set for a feast,
Decked with silver and delicate lace.
The crystal shimmered in candlelight.
A long-stemmed rose adorned each place.
But the lace was torn and stained with rust,
The roses broken and bent askew.
The plates were empty. The room was cold,
And the only guest was you.

I heard the hush of a captured bird—
The twisted wings, the pounding heart.
I saw a fisherman take a knife
And carve his gleaming catch apart.
I watched the spider weave its web.
It sparkled in the beaded dew.
But when the moth lay in its trap,
I saw the prey was you.

I came down a stair to a bolted door.
I touched the lock, and it fell away.
I found a vast and sunless room.
I wanted to leave but had to stay.
The room was a chapel lit by candles,
But the cross had been broken in two.
The priest held a chalice of blood in his hands,
And on the altar—was you.

ERIC
Ellen, poor Ellen, it was just a dream.

ELLEN
But what if it comes true? I'm so afraid.

ERIC
Only a dream.

ELLEN
O Eric, I'm afraid.

ERIC

Forget your nightmares, darling.
Today you wake to find our happiness.
I have found work. No, more than work—our future!
I have a job in Skuller's counting house.
A chance at partnership. I start at once.
This is no dream.

ELLEN
O Eric, is it true?

HARDING & MARTHE *(in unison)*
A chance at partnership.

ELLEN
What will you do?

ERIC
I am an agent selling property.
I deal with the nobility.

HARDING & MARTHE *(in unison)*
The nobility.

ELLEN
Selling property!

HARDING
To the nobility.

ELLEN
Let's celebrate! Tonight I'll make us all
A dinner fit for your nobility—
A roasted chicken, onion dumplings, cake ...

ERIC
My love, we'll have to put off celebrating.
I must set out tonight for Hungary.
The evening coach departs at six o'clock.

ELLEN
Tonight? You leave tonight? No, Eric, no!

ERIC
Don't worry, Ellen. I shall soon be back.

ELLEN
Don't leave tonight. I am afraid for you.

ERIC
I leave tonight. I have a job to do.

Harding and Marthe have been whispering between themselves since the couple began to argue. They move to the door and start to take their leave.

MARTHE
Excuse us, please. We really must be going.

HARDING
You need some privacy to talk things over.
Congratulations, Eric, on your job.

MARTHE
Good-bye. Good-bye.

HARDING
Congratulations, son.

HARDING & MARTHE

(leaving)

Good-bye . . . good-bye . . . good-bye.

Ellen watches the door close, then turns to Eric.

Duet: The Warning

ELLEN

Don't go away tonight.
Stay with me here.
I don't ask for myself.
It is for you I fear.

Don't leave me here alone
Not knowing where you've gone—
To wake with only nightmares
In a cold bed each dawn.

Don't step into that coach.
This journey is a curse.
I saw it in my dream.
The horses pull your hearse.

Don't ask me how I know it.
Don't ridicule my fright.
But I know you're in danger.
You must not leave tonight.

ERIC

What are you saying, Ellen?
You know that I can't stay.
Our future is at stake.
We're ruined by delay.

Would you make me give up
My one chance for success
And let a childish dream
Prevent our happiness?

You're still weak with fever
Your mind upset by fear.
I won't leave you alone.
Your sister will stay here.

There is no need to worry.
There is no cause for fright.
You must get some rest,
And I must leave tonight!

ELLEN *(pleading)*
Can I do nothing then to make you stay?

ERIC
I'd stay here gladly if you needed me,
But what you need is what I go to find.
Don't worry, love.
We will not be apart for long.

ELLEN
Apart? We'll never be apart!
We are man and wife. We are one flesh.
I heard the priest who married us
Describe the sacrament in just those words.
He spoke the truth!

Aria: Ellen's Vow

Flesh of my flesh, heart of my heart,
Nothing on earth can tear us apart.
No place so remote, no journey so far
That I will not be wherever you are.

I am the shadow striding beside you.
I am the sun that rises to guide you,
The seaward breeze that speeds your way,
The moonlit night that eases your day.

If you collapse on blistering sands,
I am cool water to cup in your hands.
If trapped in waves of the shipwrecking sea,
I rise like a dolphin to carry you free.

Blood of my blood, breath of my breath,
Together in joy, sorrow, or death,
My spirit is with you and surrounds you like air.
Wherever you journey, I will be there.

ERIC

O Ellen, my magnificent dear Ellen!
Still dreaming. But you've never had a dream
So marvelous. No wonder that I love you.
You will be with me always on this journey.

ELLEN

Rushing to a nearby chest of drawers, she finds a tiny portrait in a silver locket.

Wait a moment. I have something for you.
Take this little portrait of me with you,
The miniature I gave you at our wedding.
Wear it on this locket. Keep it with you.

She carefully places the locket around his neck. They stand silent for a moment.

ERIC

Come to me, darling. It's nearly time to go.

ELLEN

Hold me for a moment. Don't go yet.
I know I'm foolish, but I feel as if
I'll never hold you in my arms again.
I need this moment to remember you.
How hard it is to say good-bye, my love,
Like saying farewell to all love and joy.

ERIC

We are not saying good-bye to each other—
Only farewell to poverty and sorrow.

Good-bye to worry,
Farewell to doubt,
To scraping along,
And doing without.

Good-bye to debt
And bending to borrow,
To lying awake,
And fearing tomorrow.

Good-bye to poverty,
Hunger, and fright.
Those are the only
Farewells tonight.

Tonight our life begins! Now come and kiss me.

ELLEN

Come back to me, my love. Come back to me.
O Eric, I'm afraid! My dream still haunts me.

ERIC

Then dream with me about our happiness.
Farewell to sorrow! Tonight our life begins.

Duet Finale: The Lovers' Vow

ERIC

Flesh of my flesh, heart of my heart,
Nothing on earth can keep us apart.
No place so remote, no journey so far,
That I will not be wherever you are.

You are the shadow striding beside me.
You are the sun that rises to guide me.

ELLEN

The seaward breeze that speeds your way.
The moonlit night that eases your day.

ERIC

If I collapse on blistering sands . . .

ELLEN

I am cool water to cup in your hands.

ERIC

If trapped in waves of the shipwrecking sea . . .

TOGETHER

I rise like a dolphin to carry you free.

Blood of my blood, breath of my breath.
Together in joy, sorrow, and death,
My spirit is with you and surrounds you like air.
Wherever you journey, I will be there.

ELLEN

(suddenly disturbed)

The night has grown so cold—I've started trembling—
Cold as a tomb.
Hold me a moment. I'm so very cold.

Fade to black.

The Castle

The dining hall of Count Orlock's castle at dusk. Eric has been waiting for his host's appearance all afternoon. Two servants in ancient livery attend him, but they remain silent throughout. The room, though once grand, now is joyless and dirty. A crystal flask of red wine and a single glass sit on the table in front of Eric. Through the windows we see the deepening colors of sunset.

ERIC *(to himself)*
How dull to sit all day and watch the sun go down.
This house is dark and silent as the grave.

He now addresses the servants, who ignore him.

Where is the Count? Has he been told I'm here?
We have important business to discuss.
Hello! Can any of you understand me?

He sullenly pours himself another glass of wine.

Oh, Ellen, how I wish I'd never come.

The servants slowly proceed to draw the drapes against the night and then light candles. Eric watches their ritual with undisguised annoyance. The servants leave the room by a side exit. The main doorway then opens slowly revealing Count Orlock—a tall, thin man in his late sixties. He looks at Eric for a moment before speaking.

ORLOCK
I am Count Orlock. How considerate of you
To wait all afternoon. I was detained.
I welcome you to my ancestral home.

ERIC

(bowing slightly)

It is an honor, Count, to visit you.

ORLOCK

I trust my servants have looked after you.

ERIC

Your hospitality has been superb.

ORLOCK

You cannot know
How long I have looked forward to this evening.
I trust you have the contract I must sign.

ERIC

(taking out the papers)

Oh yes. It is the purpose of my trip.
Let me explain the details of . . .

ORLOCK
No need.

ERIC

The house has some unusual . . .

ORLOCK
No mind.

ERIC

We feel the purchase price is . . .

ORLOCK
Of course.

ERIC
I've brought along the deeds of title . . .

ORLOCK
                                        Please.
I trust you totally. What must I sign?

Eric hands him the papers and points to the places requiring the Count's signature. One by one the Count signs the papers. Finally, he closes the folio and addresses Eric.

Now you must have a drink to celebrate.

ERIC
But won't you join me?

ORLOCK
            I cannot drink wine,
So you must have a second glass for me.

ERIC

He pours himself another glass and then toasts the Count.

Yes, gladly. *Prosit, mein geerhter Graf!*
Do you intend to visit your new house
In the near future?

ORLOCK
I leave tomorrow night.

ERIC
So soon?

ORLOCK
I long to put this place behind me.

ERIC
You wish to travel?

ORLOCK
No, to leave forever.

ERIC
You'd leave your family lands? Your history?
Forsake your patrimony, your estates?

ORLOCK
I am the last survivor of my house.
You cannot understand how heavily the past
Weighs down on me. You are too young, my friend.
You are—forgive me—not of noble blood.
You cannot know the price of living on—
How ancient deeds imprison us forever.

ERIC
You don't think you will miss your own estates?

Aria: Orlock's Legacy

ORLOCK
Look at the land my fathers fought
To conquer and to own.
The towns are empty and the roads
Untraveled and overgrown.

The wind blows over barren farms.
The cottage doors swing free.
The only creatures in the field—
Crows in a leafless tree.

The woods are silent night and day,
The game all hunted down.
Only the dust and dark inherit
Forest, field, and town.

How can I leave my native land?
My patrimony is gone.

I rule a kingdom of the dead.
I perish or move on.

Coda

He sings quietly to himself to the melody of the Dies Irae.

The day of judgment comes at last
When I shall reckon with the past
And leave behind this plundered earth.
Now comes the day of my rebirth.

Orlock's monologue has made Eric uncomfortable, but he is too nervous in the aristocrat's presence to express his confusion. Instead he slowly drains his glass of wine. The Count suddenly adopts a soothing, conciliatory tone.

ORLOCK
You seem exhausted, my young friend, and nervous.
Don't let me burden you with my own troubles.
You must be lonely here—so far from home.

ERIC
I'm newly married, sir. This trip has been
Most difficult. Ellen, I mean to say, my wife,
She has been ill.

ORLOCK
And you so far from home.

ERIC

(taking out the locket)

Before I left she gave me this small portrait . . .

ORLOCK

Ignoring the locket, he carefully refills Eric's glass.

> You should relax. Enjoy the wine. You are
> A man who can appreciate the forms
> Of the nobility.

ERIC

Thank you, my lord.

ORLOCK

Relax and taste success. Your work is done.
Surrender to the pleasures of the evening.

ERIC

(toasting)

To our success, sir!

ORLOCK

Yes, to victory.

ERIC

(flushed with the wine)

My wife will be so happy. May I show you . . . ?

ORLOCK

(again ignoring Eric's gesture and moving closer)

Now we must celebrate this victory.

ERIC

Here is the portrait . . .

ORLOCK

Give me your hand.
The moment has arrived to seal our bargain.
Come taste our victory.

ERIC

(offering the locket once more)

Here is the portrait of my new bride, Ellen.

ORLOCK

Finally seeing the portrait, the Count is transfigured.

Ellen. Your bride. Ellen.

Slowly the dark space at stage right becomes illuminated—revealing Ellen's bedroom. She is asleep in a long white nightgown, but her face is softly lit.

ERIC

Isn't she beautiful? I love this portrait.
It captures both her beauty and her soul.

ORLOCK

As the Count takes the portrait, Ellen's face stage right is lit more brightly.

It captures both her beauty and her soul.
Yes, Ellen. A new bride.

Orlock now visibly begins to cast a spell over Eric.

You've brought me more than you will ever know.
Now I will show you pleasures far beyond
The petty comforts of your daylight world.

As the Count sings, Eric seemingly becomes paralyzed.

Duet: Eric's Seduction

ORLOCK

Come to me now.
Why should you wait?
The time arrives
To consummate
The bargain that
We both desire.
You are the tinder.
I am the fire.

You ache to give
Yourself to me,
Surrender your body
Eagerly—
Blood and bone,
Heart and breath.
I am your lord.
I am your death.

ERIC

I want to leave
But I remain,
Craving the pleasure
Hidden in pain.
I fear the hands
That I desire.
Why do I ache
To touch this fire?

I long to know
The ecstasy
Of giving my body
Utterly—
Blood and bone,
Heart and breath.
You are my lord,
Though you bring death.

ORLOCK

(on the verge of attacking Eric)

> Now you are mine—forever.
> Blood and bone,
> Heart and breath.
> Forever.

ERIC

> Now I am yours—forever.
> Blood and bone,
> Heart and breath.
> Forever.

(pulling himself momentarily from his trance)

No! Ellen, Ellen, Ellen!

Ellen now wakes from sleep. She has somehow heard Eric's cry. For the remainder of the scene she will hear both Eric and Orlock, but Orlock alone will hear her. Eric cannot hear Ellen, but he feels some weak sense of her presence. He is paralyzed with fear and almost totally under Orlock's spell.

ELLEN

Eric! Where are you? I can hear you calling.

ERIC

Ellen . . . Ellen . . . Ellen. *(ever weaker)*

ELLEN

> I'm with you now, my love. You are in danger.
> I feel a dark and frightful presence closing in.

ORLOCK

He has stopped and stands almost motionless as he listens to Ellen in surprise. He senses Ellen's presence.

> Who else is here? There's someone here. Ah, yes!
> I feel you strongly now. Can it be *you*?

I knew at once when I first saw your portrait.
I knew that you were one of us.

ELLEN

But who are you? Why do you threaten us?

ORLOCK

Not you. Just this young fool.

ELLEN

Don't hurt him, please!

ORLOCK

He is unworthy of you, and his judgment
Has now been passed.

ELLEN

But who are you to judge him?
Who are you?

ORLOCK

I am the past that feeds upon the present.
I am the darkness that daylight denies.
I am the sins that you must inherit—
The final truth in a world full of lies.
I am the name that cannot be said.
I am eternal, unliving, undead.

ELLEN

What do you want from us?

ORLOCK

Life and eternity.

ELLEN

Mater Maria, ora pro nobis!
How can you hear me?

ORLOCK

Because you know the darkness in yourself.
Because you see the future in your dreams.
Because you were not born
To dwell among the deaf and dumb and blind.
For centuries I've waited for your voice.
You are the promised one. You are my bride.

ELLEN

Your bride? How can you say that? Who are you?
What is your name?

ORLOCK

     My name cannot be spoken,
Not even to my bride, but others call me
Nosferatu.

ELLEN

Nosferatu—the undead!

Duet: The Battle

(Both Ellen and Orlock address Eric.)

ORLOCK

Darkness calls you
Home to rest.
After labor
Sleep is best.
Day is struggle
Without end.
Branches break
Unless they bend.

Day is only
Half of life—
Bitter hours
Of toil and strife.

But night restores
The body's ease.
Darkness cures
The soul's disease.

ELLEN

O Eric, leave
This house of death
Where every touch
And every breath
Try to trap you
In its doom.
Don't let these walls
Become your tomb.

I see the future
Branch in two—
One path illusion,
One path true.
Your choices are
Not what they seem.
Death deceives you
With its dream.

ERIC

(still in Orlock's thrall)

Darkness calls me
Home to rest.
After labor
Sleep is best.

Trio: Finale

ELLEN	ORLOCK
Come home to me.	Stay with me.
Leave dreams behind.	Leave love behind.

Let midnight pass	Let midnight pass
And morning find	And morning find
You in my arms.	Your soul set free.
My love will keep	My touch will keep
You free from harm.	You far from pain.
With me you'll sleep—	Then you will sleep—
Sleep, softly sleep.	Sleep, deeply sleep.

ERIC

(repeating fragments from one or the other characters)

Come home to you.
Leave love behind.
Let midnight pass
And morning find
Me in your arms.
Your touch will keep
Me free from pain.
With you I'll sleep—
Sleep, softly sleep.

Eric stands motionless as Orlock closes in on him. The Count slowly attacks him. Ellen can feel she has lost the struggle. Eric cries out as Nosferatu bites his neck.

ELLEN
No, no, don't hurt him! No, don't let him die!

ORLOCK

Stopping his attack, he pauses for a moment then speaks.

I'll let him live. He is my gift to you.

Eric falls to the floor unconscious.

And now I come to claim you as my bride.

Curtain

Act Two

The Arrival

Ellen stands on the harbor wall of Wisborg looking out over the sea. There should be something in her demeanor to suggest that this is not her first visit. It is dusk. The evening star has just risen above the still-glowing sunset. Ellen muses for a moment, then makes her wish on the evening star.

Aria: Ellen's Serenade

ELLEN

Far away, far away,
First star above the sea,
Planet of love, what do you say,
First star above the sea?
Tell me, Venus, goddess bright,
Will my love come home tonight,
Come home across the sea?
I wait for you, wait for you.
When will you return?

Come to me, come to me.
Sleep in my arms tonight.
Come and see what joy will be
Found in my arms tonight.
Slip into harbor out of the sea
With silken sails beside the quay.
Stand in the moon's soft light.

Then call to me, call to me.
I wait for your return.

After a moment, Skuller enters nervously. Seeing Ellen, he affects an attitude of exaggerated courtesy.

SKULLER

Good evening, Frau Hutter. Good evening. Good evening.
An unexpected pleasure.
Taking the air? A lovely, lovely night.

He offers his arm with grotesque gallantry.

Care for a stroll? Hmm? A little stroll?

ELLEN

No thank you. I was just returning home.

SKULLER

Oh, such a shame. A lovely, lovely night.

ELLEN

I really must go now, but may I ask
If you've had any word at all from Eric?

SKULLER

No word from Eric yet. No word at all.

ELLEN

But it has been three months! The summer's gone.
Night after night I sit at home afraid.
What if there's been some accident? What if . . .
And I have had such terrifying dreams.
I almost think them real. Where is my husband?
Why have we had no word?

SKULLER

                Now, now. Don't worry.
The distances are great. The mail is slow.

If something had gone wrong, we'd surely know.
Care for a stroll?

He offers his arm again.

ELLEN *(recoiling)*
No, thank you. I must go.
It's almost dark. I am expected home.

SKULLER

(waving farewell as she leaves)

Good night, dear *Frau.*
Good night . . . Good night . . .
Good riddance!
She's finally gone!
Tonight at last
The Master comes.

Night Interlude

Skuller stands looking out to sea while the sky darkens. Time passes. A ship comes slowly into sight. It is empty and unmanned except for the solitary figure of Count Orlock, who stands near the prow. As the ship nears, we see the Count is now much younger and more vital than before. The ship stops at the dock. A gangplank descends without visible human assistance. As Count Orlock disembarks, a huge swarm of rats follows him onto the land.

SKULLER

Kneeling, Skuller whispers ecstatically.

Master.

Orlock hardly notices his servant, but he extends his hand, which Skuller kisses.

NOSFERATU
I am the traveler whom you expect.

SKULLER

How long I've waited. Finally you've come.

NOSFERATU

Now you will help me find what I require.

SKULLER

Master, I welcome you to your new home.

NOSFERATU

No, not a home. I have not come to rest.
I've come to conquer—to make a new domain,
A mandate worthy of my ancestors.
Here is the future, not the barren past.
Here is the strength and scope to be reborn.
Now go. Prepare the house for my arrival.

SKULLER

I go, my lord.

Four servants appear silently and board the ship. They unload two earth-filled coffins that they slowly carry offstage. Orlock watches them leave.

NOSFERATU

What use is immortality alone?
Ellen, my chosen one,
I know that you can hear.
I'll call to you each night
As the clock strikes twelve.
I'll call to you each night
Until you answer me,
Invite me willingly
Into your arms.

The clock tower begins to strike midnight.

Aria: Nosferatu's Nocturne

I am the image that darkens your glass,
The shadow that falls wherever you pass.
I am the dream you cannot forget,
The face you remember without having met.

I am the truth that must not be spoken,
The midnight vow that cannot be broken.
I am the bell that tolls out the hours.
I am the fire that warms and devours.

I am the hunger that you have denied,
The ache of desire piercing your side.
I am the sin you have never confessed,
The forbidden hand caressing your breast.

You've heard me inside you speak in your dreams,
Sigh in the ocean, whisper in streams.
I am the future you crave and you fear.
You know what I bring. Now I am here.

Stage darkens to blackness.

The Plague

The street outside Dr. Harding's sanitarium. Ellen and Marthe are coming to visit Eric, who has been confined there since his return. As they approach, they hear the sounds of a funeral mass ending at the neighboring church. A church bell tolls.

CHORUS *(offstage)*
Dies irae, dies illa
Solvet saeclum in favilla,
Teste David cum Sibylla.

Quantus tremor est futurus
Quando judex est venturus
Cuncta stricte discussurus.

ELLEN
Death. Everywhere death. Every day death.

MARTHE
The plague. The death ship brought it to our town.
The crew was dead. It drifted into harbor.
And every night since then, people have died.

ELLEN

Listening to the chorus, she translates their words to herself.

Day of anger, fearful day,
When fire will burn the world away
As the dreaded prophets say.

MARTHE

What are you saying?

ELLEN

Just the words they're singing.
The *Dies Irae*, the Sequence of the Dead.

CHORUS

A group of monks and mourners enter. They carry two coffins. One is a child's coffin.

Liber scriptus proferetur
In quo totum continetur
Unde mundus judicetur.

Judex ergo cum censebit,
Quidquid latet apparebit,
Nil inultum remanebit.

MARTHE

But what do the words mean?

ELLEN

A prophecy. About the Day of Judgment:

When the Judge shall mount his throne,
All dark secrets shall be shown,
And his vengeance shall be known.

MARTHE

Our judgment here.

ELLEN

But this comes not from heaven.

Concert Duet With Chorus: Dies Irae

CHORUS	ELLEN	MARTHE
Dies irae, dies illa	Day of anger . . .	. . . fearful day
Solvet saeclum in favilla	When fire will burn . . .	. . . our world away

CHORUS	TOGETHER
Teste David cum Sibylla.	As the dreaded prophets say.

CHORUS	ELLEN	MARTHE
Judex ergo cum censebit,	When the Judge . . .	. . . shall mount his throne,
Quidquid latet apparebit,	All dark secrets . . .	. . . shall be shown,

CHORUS	TOGETHER
Nil inultum remanebit.	And his vengeance shall be known.

CHORUS	ELLEN
Dona eis requiem.	Deliver us from evil, Lord.

CHORUS

(moving off)

Lacrimosa dies illa,
Qua resurget ex favilla.
Dona eis requiem.

ELLEN

This evil plague!

MARTHE

All sorrows pass. You should be giving thanks
That Eric has returned.

ELLEN

But he's so sick.

They turn to the doorway of the sanitarium. As they open it, the streetfront rises to reveal the interior of the hospital ward, which they now enter. Dr. Harding meets them. A few inmates wander the periphery of the room—quietly insane.

HARDING

Dear ladies, welcome. Good that you are here.
Your Eric's getting stronger every day.

ELLEN

That is good news. How is his mind?

HARDING

He suffers from a strange delusion.
He thinks his travels left him rich,
And that the clinic is his mansion.
Be patient. Science will find a cure.
Wait here. I'll bring him.

Harding goes offstage. While she waits, Ellen watches an inmate who stands in the corner slowly rocking his head and humming as if he were hearing some secret music.

ELLEN

Marthe, I'm afraid.

The doctor returns with Eric who wears white hospital clothes. He is pale and nervous but also oddly self-possessed. Eric is accompanied by Skuller, who is also now an inmate of the asylum. When he enters, Skuller acts as if he were Eric's servant.

ERIC

Ellen, my love!
O why did no one tell me you were here?
These new servants are all worthless. *(to Skuller)* Worthless!

ELLEN

O Eric, I'm so happy to be here!

ERIC

If that is true, why have you stayed away
After I bought this splendid house for you?
You leave me here alone—leave me with servants.

(to Skuller)

Now get away, you worthless layabout!
I want to speak in private with my wife.

Skuller retreats bowing and smiling with exaggerated politeness. Harding is obviously embarrassed by the conversation. He confers with Marthe.

HARDING

I think that we should give them time alone.

Skuller herds the patients back into the ward. Harding leads Marthe away separately.

ERIC

We're finally alone. O Ellen,
Come back to me. I miss you so.
I am so lonely in this house.

ELLEN

I haven't left you. I visit every day.

ERIC

What mockery! Your little visits!
Why don't you live here in our home?
Why don't we live as man and wife?

ELLEN

How can I live here in a hospital?
Eric, you are ill. You need to rest.

ERIC

What nonsense! All I need is you.
I want you here. You are my wife.
I want you . . . want you . . . Ellen . . .

He becomes faint and staggers. Ellen rushes to support him. They sit together on the waiting-room bench.

ELLEN

Just rest a moment here beside me.

ERIC

Yes, I am tired. So deathly tired.
I've hardly slept since I returned—
Such nightmares. Endless nightmares.

ELLEN

But we are safe together now.

ERIC

My journey made us very rich,
But it was hard and dangerous.
I dream about it every night.

ELLEN

But now your nightmares are all passed.

ERIC

Some nightmares never go away.

Aria: Eric's Mad Song

I sailed a ship
In the storm-wracked sea,
And all were drowned
Except for me.
I swam all night
Through death-cold waves
Till my shipmates called
From their sunken graves,
A lucky life for you, lad, a lucky life for you!

I fought through wars
In a barren land
Till none were left
Of my rugged band.
On a field of dead
Only I stood free.
Then a blind crow laughed
From a blasted tree,
A lucky life for you, lad, a lucky life for you!

I scaled a mountain
Of cold sharp stone.
The others fell,
And I climbed alone.
When I reached the top,
The winds were wild,
But a skull at my feet
Looked up and smiled,
A lucky life for you, lad, a lucky life for you!

Now I sit in my mansion
With my art and my gold,
And a dozen servants
Who do what they're told,
But the nights are long,
And dawn brings no cheer,
And I wake alone,
And the paintings all sneer,
A lucky life for you, lad, a lucky life for you!

The agitation of Eric's song draws Harding, Skuller, and the assistants back into the room. Concerned by Eric's excited state, they start to take him back into the ward.

ERIC

What do you want? Am I expected somewhere?

ELLEN

O Doctor, let him stay a moment more.

Harding gestures apologetically but continues to lead Eric away.

ERIC

Forgive me, dear. I have appointments elsewhere.
Farewell.

(leaving)

I am so lonely in this house.

Ellen stands impassively as Eric is led away. She is left alone onstage with Skuller,
who slowly approaches her.

SKULLER

He was a very promising young man.
You know, of course, that he will not recover.

ELLEN

You hideous fool! Your greed destroyed him.

SKULLER

I did what must be done.
Eric was very lucky—
Lucky to play his part,
Lucky to be alive.
But you're the only one
Who matters now.

ELLEN

What do you mean?

SKULLER

You hear the Master call each night.

ELLEN

I don't know what you're speaking of.

SKULLER

O please don't lie to me, dear lady.
You hear the Master call each night.
When will you answer him?

(*Ellen is silent.*)

When?

ELLEN (*softly*)

Never.

SKULLER

It's pointless to resist. He is too strong.
Soon you will love the Master as I do.

ELLEN

Love him? I have refused to answer him.

SKULLER

He is immortal and invincible.

ELLEN

If that is so, why does he wait and court me?

SKULLER

You must come willingly to be his bride.

ELLEN

But I will never willingly be his.

SKULLER

A woman never knows what she might do.

ELLEN

I know what I will do. I will destroy him.

SKULLER

There's only one way to destroy the Master.

ELLEN

Tell me what it is.

SKULLER

Come closer and I will.

Ellen comes next to him.

He rules the night. He does not rule the day.

ELLEN

What does that mean? You're just tormenting me.

SKULLER

Oh, yes, I know a way, but one
Too dangerous and lewd for you—
A way a woman might attempt.

ELLEN

What is the way?

SKULLER

Come closer still, and I will tell you.

Ellen leans closer to him and he whispers to her.

If she could hold him spellbound until dawn,
He would be caught by daylight unawares,
Far from his coffin and his native earth,
Then he would vanish into smoke and ashes.

ELLEN

If she could hold him spellbound until dawn . . . .

TOGETHER

Then he would be destroyed.

Skuller suddenly kisses her. She recoils, and he laughs wildly.

SKULLER

> It will not happen.
> If you encounter him, you will surrender—
> Like me. Like all the others. You will see.
> Like me. Like all the others . . .

He leaves, talking to himself. Ellen is now alone.

ELLEN

> What is there left to choose except my death?
> Why should the darkness not be brought to light?

Fade to black.

Midnight

Ellen is alone in her apartment. She stands by the large open window looking out over the moonlit roofs of the town. She seems momentarily lost in a deep trance as if she were in communion with some unseen and disturbing presence. She has finally answered Orlock's call, and she knows he is about to arrive. A distant church bell strikes midnight.

ELLEN

(talking to herself with increasing anxiety)

Midnight!

No one near,
No one knowing,
No one to help me.
He is coming.
I must pray—
Pray to the Virgin.
She will help me.

Aria: Ellen's Prayer

Ellen prays the Salve Regina, *first in Latin, then in her own words.*

> *Salve, Regina,*
> *Mater misericordiae*
> *Vita dulcedo*
> *Et spes nostra, salve.*
> *Ad te clamamus*

Exules filii Evae.
Ad te suspiramus
Gementes et flentes
In hac lacrimarum valle . . .

Ellen breaks down in mid-prayer and begins again, mistranslating the words in a way that reflects her state of mind.

Salve, Regina,
Queen of the heavens—
Star of the evening,
Star of the sea.

Mother of mercy,
Mother of misery,
Hear me, my light,
My life, and my hope.

Virgin, who crushed
The serpent, protect me—
An orphan, an exile,
A daughter of Eve.

Mother of sorrow,
Guide me through darkness,
Lend me strength
In this valley of tears.

Salve, Maria,
Mother of misery,
Mother of mercy,
Save me from evil.

Trapped and defenseless,
I reach for your grace.
But I see only darkness
And death's graven face.

She suddenly senses Nosferatu's approach.

Nosferatu! He is here.
Death stands in the street.
Death waits at the door.

She tries to pray again.

> *Salve, Regina. Mater . . .*
> *Ad te clamamus . . . filia.*
> He is climbing the stairs!
> *Mater Maria . . . Mater . . . Mater!*

Her fear turns to resolution.

> Now comes the test of justice.
> Holy Virgin, help me send
> Death himself down to the dead.

Ellen rushes to the window and pulls the heavy curtains shut. She then stands in the middle of the room silently looking at the doorway. The door opens slowly to reveal Orlock at the threshold. As he stands there motionless for a moment, his shadow stretches forward into the room.

NOSFERATU
I who command must ask to enter.
You have invited me?

ELLEN
Yes. Enter.

NOSFERATU
At last I see you face-to-face.

ELLEN
And I see you.

NOSFERATU *(drawing nearer)*
At last the spirit finds its flesh.
My soul has called to you each night.
At last you answer.

ELLEN
I had no choice.

NOSFERATU
I offer you a choice tonight
No living woman ever had.
I offer immortality.

ELLEN
You promise life, but you are death.

NOSFERATU
No, I am life. Eternal life.

ELLEN
Life without love. Life without God.

NOSFERATU
I am a god—eternal, strong.

ELLEN
A god of evil, a god of death!

NOSFERATU
A god who lives by his own laws.

ELLEN
I cannot choose to love this god.

NOSFERATU
You are too young to understand
How little comes to us by choice.
We are not here tonight to choose
But to fulfill a prophecy.
The only reason we were born
Was to be here together now—
This night, this room, this bed.

ELLEN *(to herself)*

My marriage bed!

NOSFERATU

Now understand. Whatever it is
We choose tonight, we choose together—
Eternal life, eternal death.

He takes her by the wrists, and they look at each other.

ELLEN

I am afraid—of you,
Afraid of my own dreams.

NOSFERATU

Do you not understand, my love,
That I, too, am afraid?
I have imagined you for centuries
And yet tonight the hand
I offer you is trembling.
There's nothing in the world
That can destroy me—except you.
We live together or we die.

ELLEN

How can I love you?

NOSFERATU

You will love me when you know yourself,
You whom the world considers weak and frail.

Aria: Nosferatu's Vision

You are the moon in a sunlit sky—
Pale, diminished, alone.
All of your life you have traveled toward
The night you have never known.

I am the darkness that falls from the sky,
The blackness that brings you light,
He who reveals your one true form—
Cold, eternal, and bright.

He takes her by the arms and looks at her intently.

How can you say you do not feel desire?

ELLEN
I cannot tell you what I feel.
I feel
Everything and nothing.

NOSFERATU
And how could it be otherwise?
You do not know your own desire.

Duet: The Final Proposition

NOSFERATU	ELLEN
You are the moon.	I am the moon.
I am the night,	You are the night,
My darkness draws	Your darkness brings
Your secrets to light.	My secrets to light.
Out of your pain	Out of my pain
Emerges delight.	Emerges delight.
All of your life	All of my life
Has led to this night.	Has led to this night.
Your daylight world	The daylight world
Fosters illusion.	Fosters illusion.
Only my kiss	Only your kiss
Ends your confusion.	Ends my confusion.
Only the darkness	Only the darkness
Makes the moon bright.	Makes the moon bright.
All of your life	All of my life
Has led to this night.	Has led to this night.

NOSFERATU

Now while the world sleeps, you must awaken
To your new life. It must be done tonight.

ELLEN

It must be done tonight.

NOSFERATU

You will be mine before the dawn.

ELLEN

Before the dawn.

NOSFERATU

Now is the time—this room, this night, this bed.

ELLEN

Now is the time.

NOSFERATU

How long I've waited for
This night, this room, this bed.
How long I've ached to touch
Your arms, your lips, your hair.
And you were waiting, too—
Waiting unaware.

ELLEN

But now the night has come.

NOSFERATU

Now we are not alone.
We have eternity
To taste each other's flesh,
To know each other's soul.

ELLEN

We have eternity.

NOSFERATU

Now you are mine.
You are mine—forever.

ELLEN

I shall be yours,
Yours—forever.

But let me spend one moment
To look around this room,
To look at my old life
One final time before
I say good-bye forever.
How many mornings I
Awoke in this dear bed.
How many mornings I
Lay here—enfolded safe
Within my Eric's arms . . .

NOSFERATU *(interrupting)*

Your old life—an illusion, a dream!

ELLEN

My old life—an illusion, a dream.

NOSFERATU

Now I shall bring you
To your true life.
Now you are mine—forever.

He pushes her down on the bed and slowly bends down to attack her.

ELLEN *(surrendering to him)*

Yes, I am yours—forever.

Holding her in his arms, Nosferatu bites into her neck in a slow but passionate way. Moment by moment, Ellen loses strength. The church bells ring.

> NOSFERATU *(looking up)*
> The morning bells! The night is over.
> What have you done?

> ELLEN
> The night is over.
> And I am yours—
> Yours forever.

She staggers over to the windows and pulls the drapes apart. Morning light streams into the room.

> Yes, I am yours forever—
> Yours in death.

She collapses, dead. Nosferatu stands transfixed by the light. He starts to turn away but deliberately turns back to face the window and is slowly destroyed. Moments later Harding and Marthe enter the room and stare in bewildered terror at Ellen's body.

Curtain

Sotto Voce

Notes on the Libretto as a Literary Form

for
Herbert Lindenberger

sotto voce: Italian for "under the voice."
A direction in vocal music to sing barely
audibly, an aside.

I.

*The poet of the opera house and the idiot
were at a certain time synonymous among
the learned of London.*

—Lorenzo Da Ponte (1819)

No major poetic genre in English currently ranks lower in general literary esteem than the opera libretto. It occupies a position of opprobrium below even
obscure and discarded forms like pastoral eclogue or verse sermon. A contemporary reader may have no opinion on the status of the mock epic, but he or
she will probably be well stocked with specific objections to the libretto. It is a
truth we hold self-evident, at least in the English-speaking world, that the verbal component of opera is sub-literary—full of implausible plotting, hyperbolic characterization, absurd transitions, and incompetent versification. It
will not occur to most detractors, however, that they have never read a complete libretto in its original language but only (if they have read one at all) in a
poor, antiquated, and severely cut translation. A few scholars may celebrate the
rich traditions of operatic theater, but for the general reader the libretto remains synonymous with bad poetry and stilted drama.

Opera began, however, as a literary project—the attempt in 1597 by the
Florentine Camerata, a group of artists and intellectuals, to recreate the performance practices of classical Greek drama. The poetic text was primary. The ac-
companying music was simplified from the prevailing manner, which was intricately polyphonic, into a simpler, monodic style designed to project and
underscore the verse. The earliest operas were not based on singing so much as
poetic declamation. It is significant that the text of *Dafne,* the first opera, survives while the music has been lost.

No one comes to the opera to hear the libretto; nor has any work of musical
drama ever maintained a place in the repertory solely on the basis of its text.

While opera is indisputably a type of drama, it is preeminently musical theater in which the composer now exercises controlling interest. The Renaissance debate on *prima la musica o prima le parole*? (Does music take precedence or do the words?) has been settled by posterity.

But must one medium inevitably dominate the other in a collaborative art form? The philosopher Susanne K. Langer believed that every work of art "has its being in only one order of art; compositions of different orders are not simply conjoined, but all except one will cease to appear as what they are." When two or more arts collaborate, one art form does not merely dominate, it subsumes the others. "Music ordinarily swallows words and action creating (thereby) opera, oratorio, or song." Opera is, Langer asserts, unavoidably a composer's art.

If music takes precedence in opera, the historical record nonetheless demonstrates the crucial importance of the libretto. Composers almost inevitably create their best work when given their best texts. Mozart's three most widely esteemed operas—*Don Giovanni, Le Nozze di Figaro,* and *Così Fan Tutte*—all have superb libretti by the same poet, Lorenzo Da Ponte. Vincenzo Bellini worked almost exclusively with Felice Romani whose elegant verse spurred him, the composer maintained, to his best music. If one surveys the thousands of Italian operas produced in what William Weaver has called the "Golden Century" between Rossini and Puccini, one will be astonished to note that the majority of the works still regularly performed have libretti by only five poets—Felice Romani, Salvatore Cammarano, Francesco Maria Piave, Arrigo Boito, and Luigi Illica. Great librettists seem rarer than great composers. Likewise, it is significant how the single opera that survives in the international repertory by productive composers like Ponchielli, Catalani, Giordano, Mascagni, and Leoncavallo is inevitably also the score based on what is conspicuously each composer's best libretto. *Prima la musica,* but the best operatic music depends on being called into existence by the right words.

If the poet is the subordinate partner in opera, the librettist nonetheless has often been the decisive provocateur of artistic change. The great "reform" of tragic opera, which earned Christoph Willibald Gluck his central place in the history of the form and created masterpieces like *Orfeo ed Euridice* (1762) and *Alceste* (1767), was the idea of his librettist, Ranieri de'Calzabigi. (Calzabigi even served as ghostwriter for Gluck's famous manifesto on reforming opera.) Likewise Hugo von Hofmannsthal's innovative libretti induced Richard Strauss to explore aspects of both music and theater the composer might otherwise have ignored. A few decades later Bertolt Brecht decisively shaped Kurt Weill's musical career with his unorthodox libretti that mixed classical, cabaret, and avant-garde elements. Since the words come first, they have the potential to lead the music into new artistic territory.

As opera developed, however, so did the role of the words. In his *Vie de Rossini* (1824) Stendhal speculated that one reason for the international success of Italian opera was that the foreign audience needed to understand only a few words or phrases from an aria to apprehend its meaning. The music did the rest. Opera still depended on drama, but poetry was no longer a necessary component for an audience increasingly made up of foreigners.

Watching Rossini's operas, Stendhal also noted a significant shift in the expressive relation between words and music. Rossini's melodies no longer focused explicitly on projecting the complete poetic text. Instead his music concerned itself with creating a total dramatic effect in which the poetry was only one element. "In other words," writes musicologist Rodolfo Celletti, "significant melody gives significance even to words which in and of themselves do not have it." The composer not only underscores the meaning of the text; he also adds a resonant subtext to words and phrases that do not necessarily have evocative power on the page.

Each time that Violetta repeats the words *"E strano"* ("It's strange") in *La Traviata,* Verdi's music evocatively recapitulates her emotional history. Verdi eventually made this notion of key words and phrases central to his dramatic planning. He sometimes designed whole acts around *sceniche parole* (pictorial words), which served the same thematic function in his operas as leitmotifs did in Wagner's. The dramatic effect of such musical devices proved so strong—and their employment so enduringly useful—that it changed the librettist's function in a small but significant way. Endowed by music with special meaning, the phrase became more important than the line or stanza. The poet still provided the composer with the text, but the poet now was increasingly unable to shape its subtext.

Once music became the ascendant element in opera, the role of the librettist decisively changed. As Patrick J. Smith comments in *The Tenth Muse* (1970), his astute historical study of the libretto, this shift "necessitated a different evaluation of the qualities of a librettist, for he no longer was primarily a poet to be judged by the musicality of his lines and aptness of his rhythms, rhymes, and similes. The librettist had become more: he had become a dramatist as well. . . . To consider the librettist merely a poet is to denigrate his function in the creation of an opera, for in the vast majority of cases the librettist supplied the original, motive force for the composition of the opera and created the dramatic node around which the final work was constructed."

II.

Literature, in the form of the text to be set to music,
must always be ready to help the composer; whether
music can help literature is another matter.

—Anthony Burgess (1991)

Opera is the only living form of poetic drama—the last corner of theater in which the poet remains a necessary collaborator. Although opera has declined in influence and vitality over the past century, it continues to thrive and develop as an art form—supported by a large and famously devoted international audience. Hundreds of contemporary operas, including many premieres, are produced each year with a majority of them still written entirely or partially in verse. Opera is also the only surviving form of contemporary tragic theater. If a contemporary poet wants to write verse tragedy, he or she has only two practical alternatives—translate the classics or write for the opera house.

If a poet wishes to write a libretto seriously, however, he or she must accept that opera is not considered primarily a literary form. The poet may remain a necessary partner in creating a new opera, but he or she is indisputably a subordinate one, and poetry itself is secondary to other literary concerns in a libretto. "The job of the librettist," wrote W. H. Auden, "is to furnish the composer with a plot, characters and words: of these, the least important so far as the audience is concerned, are the words." There is nothing to stop a writer from filling a libretto with superb poetry, but the task can only be done while simultaneously meeting a formidable set of compositional and theatrical demands that have nothing to do with poetic excellence.

How then does one judge the quality of an opera libretto? Is it to be read as poetry or drama? Need it have any genuine existence as a verbal work of art? Or do the words serve only as a dramatic framework for the composer? There are no universal answers. What matters ultimately is the unique chemistry between each poet and composer. Different texts call different sorts of operas into existence. Maurice Maeterlinck's *Pelléas et Mélisande* would probably not have been a viable text for Puccini or Prokofiev, but it proved ideal for Claude Debussy. Part of a great opera composer's genius is the ability to find or instigate the right libretto. In a few cases—preeminently that of Richard Wagner—that has meant writing the libretti himself.

The true test of a libretto is ultimately how well it operates in the finished work of art. It cannot fairly be judged separately from the musical drama it inspires because its purpose was specifically to create that *Gesamtkunstwerk*. Viewed solely as a literary work, Boito's libretto for Verdi's *Otello*—although fine Italian verse— is surely inferior to Shakespeare's tragedy. Verdi's operatic setting, however, seems fully equal to Shakespeare's play. A libretto, therefore, cannot be meaningfully judged on verbal quality alone. Opera's material essence is primarily sound, but words represent only a narrow part of that sonic dimension.

Yet some libretti exist satisfactorily on the page. Pietro Metastasio and Bertolt Brecht, for example, both wrote libretti that can be read solely for their literary merit. Such achievement is not mandatory for a librettist, but in an otherwise successfully realized musical drama, good poetry adds an imaginative frisson that amplifies the work's expressive effect.

W. H. Auden's *Paul Bunyan* (1941) probably reads better than it performs—despite Benjamin Britten's inspired score—because the text succeeds more conspicuously as poetry than drama. The brilliance of Auden's verse may even highlight the libretto's inadequacy as theater. By comparison, Auden and Chester Kallman's text for Hans Werner Henze's *The Bassarids* (1966), which was based on Euripides' *The Bacchae,* contains little significant poetry, but it works powerfully in performance as musical drama. The difference between the two libretti cannot be seen as accidental. If one reads all of Auden's libretti in chronological order, one sees the authorial attention shift from poetic considerations to dramatic ones. The implications of Auden's development are clear. The most distinguished English-language librettist of the twentieth century eventually considered poetry a secondary consideration in creating an opera.

Another libretto that reads brilliantly on the page is Ronald Duncan's still controversial text for Benjamin Britten's *The Rape of Lucretia* (1946). Freely based on a now forgotten French play by André Obey, Duncan's libretto is poetically distinguished, dramatically powerful, thematically rich, and theatrically innovative—offering a level of complexity perfectly suited to the intimacy of a chamber opera. A student of F. R. Leavis and protégé of Ezra Pound, Duncan had played an important part—along with T. S. Eliot and Christopher Fry—in the British revival of verse drama after World War II. *The Rape of Lucretia* was a critical success but a financial failure. Britten, who had composed a beautiful but astringent score, soon blamed his librettist, who had been attacked at great length by one influential reviewer. Duncan was abruptly dropped from the composer's inner circle, and replaced by another librettist for future projects. While it may be that the particular virtues of Duncan's text were not ideally suited to Britten's talents, the libretto remains one of the finest written in the twentieth century. Although *The Rape of Lucretia* has gradually earned a place in the international repertory, little credit is given to Duncan's libretto, which most critics still ignore or censure—parroting the composer's early complaints. In opera, such are the rewards of poetic excellence and innovation.

III.

Composers should throw out most of their words.

—Joaquin Nin-Culmell (2000)

Opera demands immense narrative compression. It lacks the novel's ability to communicate the duration of time. It cannot portray complex linear narrative as easily as film. What opera excels at is presenting peak moments of human emotion. While the structure of opera is narrative, its power is lyric. Better perhaps than any other art form, it can represent the full emotional intensity of a specific moment, especially from the subjective perspective of a particular character. That special lyric intensity explains why people so often cry at the opera, even at the performances of works they have known for years. For a few moments they have become the character on the stage. That imaginary figure's sufferings have become their own. Composers and librettists have understood that this transforming subjectivity is not incidental but essential to opera's identity. "Opera," Bellini wrote, "through singing, must make one weep, shudder, die." The librettist creates and arranges the dramatic action to pass from one such lyric episode to another, always leading to new climaxes. Balance, verisimilitude, and subtlety may be virtues in a novel, but they are incidental to a libretto. Opera strives instead for lyricality, power, and emotional intensity.

Opera tends to explore the extremes of human experience, especially the limits of suffering. Tragic opera remains the only theatrical form still unabashedly committed to Aristotle's notion of emotional catharsis through pity and terror. Modern literary critics frequently lamented the "death of Tragedy" in Europe after the generation of Goethe and Schiller because as *literary* critics they rarely looked beyond spoken theater. The nineteenth century, however, was one of tragedy's greatest periods—equaled only by Sophocles' Athens or Shakespeare's London. But its most powerful and enduring tragedies were not written by Shelley, Byron, Hugo, or de Musset, but by Bellini, Donizetti, Verdi, Puccini, and Wagner.

Although opera is mostly lyric in its effect, the libretto remains dramatic in its form. The text, however poetic in its particulars, must ultimately be judged less for its verbal felicity than for the power of its plotting, the depth of its characterization, and the memorability of its dramatic situations. Psychology is not a concern that most poets bring to their verse; but in creating a compelling libretto, a gift for evocative psychological portrayal is no less necessary than facility at versification. Not meter or metaphor, but motive and melody drive opera.

The genius of the Italian libretto rests on its passionate adherence to a simple dramatic principle—that the audience does not need to be told everything for a dramatic moment to have its full emotive and imaginative effect. In a manner reminiscent of Modernist poetry, Italian libretti shape their effects as much by what they omit as by what they include.

The necessary compression of a good libretto explains why operatic plots appear disjunctive and hyperbolic to a reader of the novel. Felice Romani quite sensibly sought different effects than did his contemporary Jane Austen. Opera requires emotional clarity and immediacy, not the careful examination of motivation, sensibility, and social context that enliven the novel. Most English-language literati, unfamiliar with opera in performance and generally unable to read libretti in the original language, have rarely understood the aesthetic of opera—intellectually or experientially. "The Englishman is musical," declared George Bernard Shaw, "but he is not operatic." The same might be said of most American intellectuals. If they approve of any opera at all, they, like Shaw, usually prefer Wagner's *Ring*, which takes four evenings to unfold, moving as slowly as a novel. Whatever Wagner's many virtues, they do not include compression.

IV.

That Romani! He promises everything but hands over nothing.
—Gaetano Donizetti (1828)

The dilemma of the contemporary composer is to find a suitable collaborator. There is at present no proven tradition of writing words for opera, at least in English. Poets lack experience both in writing for the stage and composing lyrics for music. Playwrights understand dramatic structure and characterization but have rarely developed the necessary skills of extreme compression and overtly lyric language. A common mistake of contemporary composers has been to set a prose play to music. The result is usually a well-made plot and very dull music. "So many of these new operas—by words possessed!" complains Cuban-American composer Joaquin Nin-Culmell who claims that a libretto needs unusual concision and intensity to achieve what he calls "operatic speed."

Should composers write their own libretti? Enough composers have managed the task to demonstrate the virtues of single authorship. Richard Wagner, the exception to most rules in music, wrote all of his own libretti. (Poetry was only one aspect of Wagner's vision of total artistic control, which culminated in building Bayreuth, an opera house dedicated solely to the production of his own works under ideal conditions.) Sergei Prokofiev also wrote or co-

authored all his libretti. A less well-known example is Donizetti, not a conspicuously literary man, who had a real theatrical talent for comedy. He wrote hilari-
ous libretti for *La Convenienze Teatrali* and *Il Campanello* and co-authored
Don Pasquale, a comic masterpiece. (Significantly, Donizetti left the creation of
his tragic libretti to poets.) With Hector Berlioz one begins to see some of the
dangers of single authorship. He was a capable poet, but his magnificent *Les
Troyens,* which he based on Virgil's *Aeneid,* became too long and too complex
to be easily staged. Only the last three acts of *Les Troyens* were performed in
Berlioz's lifetime. An experienced librettist might have compressed the story
and situations. The literary problems of libretti written by composers, however, go beyond epic length. They usually center on lack of basic literary craft in
plotting, characterization, dialogue, and versification. Michael Tippett wrote
ambitious but awkward libretti for his mature operas, which are allusive,
mythic, and densely symbolic psychodramas. Tippett's best opera, *The Mid-
summer Marriage* (1955), which boasts a gorgeously original score, survives despite its complex and confusing text. Gian Carlo Menotti and Carlisle Floyd
have also written their own libretti, which are theatrically effective, emotionally direct, and dramatically negligible, though a few works like Floyd's *Susannah* (1955) or Menotti's *The Unicorn, the Gorgon and the Manticore* (1956),
achieve true dramatic intensity. In general, however, composers lack the literary skill or ambition to write their own words. For most composers, the issue is
not whether to collaborate but how to do so effectively.

An extended partnership seems the ideal situation in opera—if the right
partners can be joined. So many of the enduring works in the international
repertory are products of so few long-term partnerships that a critic must con-
clude that stable creative collaboration has decisive benefits. Over half of the
standard repertory (the fifty most frequently performed operas in the world)
are the work of only seven creative teams—Mozart/Da Ponte, Bellini/Romani,
Verdi/Piave, Verdi/Boito, Puccini/Illica, Strauss/Hofmannsthal, and, of course,
Wagner/Wagner. (In the English-speaking world a single team, Gilbert and
Sullivan, the only partnership in which the librettist gets top billing, holds a
virtual monopoly on the operetta repertory.) The operatic ideal, is therefore,
not merely a matter of getting a skilled librettist and composer together, but
in creating an ongoing collaboration that complements and challenges both
artists. One sees the power of such partnerships even today in works like *Nixon*

in China (1972) and *The Death of Klinghoffer* (1991) by John Adams and Alice Goodman.

V.

> ... *In short, that which is pure image,*
> *comprehensible in a pantomimic way—which is*
> *what a good opera libretto needs, for wholly a*
> *third of the words nearly always get lost.*
>
> —Richard Strauss (1928)

Mozart's two final operas are *Die Zauberflöte (The Magic Flute)* and *La Clemenza di Tito*. Although both works find the composer at the height of his power, *The Magic Flute* has universally been ranked as superior by both audiences and critics. How can this be so when *La Clemenza di Tito* contains equally great music, and Metastasio's magisterial Italian verse is indisputably finer than Emanuel Schikaneder's bumptious German libretto? *The Magic Flute*'s superiority rests on the simple fact that it provides better theater. However incompetent as a poet, Schikaneder was a consummate man of the stage. Designing a star vehicle for his own comic talents, he skillfully planned the dramatic effect of each scene and number. His episodic narrative also gave room for Masonic symbolism to occupy a more imaginatively powerful place than they could have in Metastasio's intricately planned and plotted libretto. Not all artistic innovation is entirely deliberate. Through a combination of poetic incompetence and theatrical intuition, Schikaneder unwittingly predicted the future of the libretto: as musical development made the librettist's verse less important, the poet would begin to shape the drama through the power of symbols.

By seventeen Hugo von Hofmannsthal had become famous across German-speaking Europe for his poetry—the literary *Wunderkind* of the Austro-Hungarian empire. By twenty-eight, however, he had abandoned lyric poetry. Distressed by the solipsism of modern verse and the inadequacy of language to represent the world, he turned to theater, a concrete and collaborative art, for its public and communal qualities. It was not the Realist drama of his era, however, that attracted Hofmannsthal. Instead, he imagined a symbolic theater of myth and ritual similar to Greek or medieval drama. The poet's task he felt, was to create "the myth of the time." Opera in particular fascinated him with its expressive power and ritualized action. For the rest of his life Hofmannsthal collaborated with Richard Strauss, whom he did not particularly like but respected as a composer. Together they eventually created six operas, including at least four acknowledged masterpieces, *Elektra* (1909), *Der Rosenkavalier* (1911), *Ariadne auf Naxos* (1912), and *Die Frau ohne Schatten* (1919). W. B. Yeats and T. S. Eliot underwent similar, though less extreme, artistic crises that also drew them to poetic drama for its communal and ritual qualities. In England and Ireland of the early twentieth century, however, opera was not yet a vital artistic alternative to spoken theater. There was neither the tradition nor the individual talent for serious English-language opera until Auden and Britten began their musical collaborations.

If the libretto adds enormous constraints to the poet's imagination, it also offers unusual freedoms, especially the opportunity to tell stories outside the conventions of verisimilitude. Music can make fantasy and myth, symbolism and expressionism credible. Bertolt Brecht, Gertrude Stein, Jean Cocteau, and Hugo von Hofmannsthal all successfully created experimental theatrical works in the opera house that would never have succeeded in spoken theater. The allegorical quality of Hofmannsthal's *Die Frau ohne Schatten* would have been risible without Strauss's music vividly embodying the symbols.

Modern literary criticism remains mostly centered in Romantic notions of the artist as an individual creative imagination. Consequently, notions of collaborative art remain difficult to discuss or comprehend. Collaboration seems always to imply compromise or dilution of individual vision. Great art, Romanticism suggests, requires the assertion of individuality, whatever the cost. Yet the performing arts—opera, drama, ballet, cinema, and jazz—almost inevitably require collaboration. Theater does not merely survive such partnership; the art emerges from the energy unleashed by it. Successful collaboration creates a combination not only greater than the sum of the parts but also slightly different. Neither W. S. Gilbert nor Arthur Sullivan—two abundantly talented artists—ever achieved work separately on so high a level as in their temperamental and eventually unstable partnership. Nor did Gertrude Stein or Virgil Thomson ever create individually any large work as memorable or constantly delightful as they did together in *Four Saints in Three Acts* (1937), the great Modernist masterpiece of American opera. Once combined, their idio-syncratic weaknesses became collaborative strengths.

Although opera has been popular in the United States for nearly two centuries—and in the mid-nineteenth century it was almost as popular as the movies are today—it remains a foreign art form. At the beginning of the twenty-first century, there are still no American operas established in the inter-national repertory with the possible exceptions of Gian Carlo Menotti's slight one-act Christmas TV special, *Amahl and the Night Visitors* (1951) and George Gershwin's "folk opera," *Porgy and Bess* (1935), which contains spoken dialogue and resembles a Broadway musical. More significant and shameful, there are still no native works in the standard repertory of American opera houses. Go to Vienna, St. Petersburg, Budapest, or Barcelona, and one finds rich reperto-ries of national works. These operas may not be international favorites, but they occupy important places in local affection and esteem. In America a few works hold a precarious position—Menotti's *The Medium* (1946), Carlisle Floyd's *Susannah* (1955), Samuel Barber's *Vanessa* (1958), and perhaps two or three others. These works rarely appear in our major houses (as national op-eras do in Europe) but survive mainly in student productions at colleges or conservatories. One is still more likely to see *Porgy and Bess* in Germany than in the United States. Our musical intelligentsia, moreover, either openly dislikes or condescends to these works, which are all tonal and melodic. Such is the cultural situation an American composer and librettist face in creating new operas—indifference, contempt, or at best condescension.

VI.

Opera is the last refuge of the High Style.
—W. H. Auden (1967)

Gluck's vision of opera assumed collaboration so close that neither art could be judged or even examined separately from the other. "The union between the words and the singing must be so close that the poem does not seem less made to fit the music than the music to fit the poem." Gluck's theory is persuasive in the abstract, but by presenting an Olympian view of an ideal *completed* work, it offers little practical guidance to a poet beginning a libretto.

Creating words for opera, the poet faces different demands than in writing for the page. The poet must not only write to satisfy his or her own literary vision, but also to meet specific needs of the audience, the singers, and the composer.

"The first duty of the librettist," wrote Auden and Kallman, "is, needless to say, to write verses which excite the musical imagination of the composer; if these verses should also possess poetic merit in themselves, so much the better, but such merit is a secondary consideration." This formulation neatly captures the serious poet's dilemma. The crucial audience for a libretto is not the reader or the operagoer but the composer, and the poetic text exists not to survive as words but to be transformed into another medium. Sometimes that transformation is violent. While composing *Aida*, Verdi sent his librettist Antonio Ghislanzoni a radically cut and changed version of one scene. "I know what you will say," wrote the composer, "'and what has become of verse, rhyme, and stanza?' I don't know what to answer you. I only know that whenever the action demanded it, I would at once abandon rhythm, rhyme, and stanza."

The language of an opera libretto is by necessity less densely textured than verse written for the page. The poet must make the verse more direct and transparent for both practical and artistic reasons. In practical terms, the poet must write words that the audience can understand when set to music—lines that under the worst circumstances, can register dramatically—even when every word is not audible. For purely artistic reasons a poet must also create less densely textured verse for a libretto because in opera the words need not communicate everything in themselves. The words, in fact, need to leave room for the composer. (It cannot be coincidental that all of the enduring operas based on Shakespeare have been done in foreign languages.) While the poet creates—or at least initiates—the story, characters, situations, and sentiments of the drama, it is the composer who brings them alive on stage. The poet's challenge is to provide the composer with enough depth but not too much detail.

But what is enough and not too little? The composer may ultimately understand the right verbal texture better than the poet. Those big, bold lines that seem most shamefully naked to a poet are often those that the composer instinctively knows how to clothe most magnificently in music. By contrast, it is sometimes the least important lines that need to be most intricately written since no powerful musical idea will support them.

Meanwhile the singers place an additional dramatic demand on the librettist. The performers need to understand at all times what their characters are thinking and feeling. A poet writing a libretto is not primarily creating lines of verse but summoning up characters who in the situations depicted would believably speak those lines. To this effort, the composer then makes it emotionally credible—indeed inevitable—that the characters would sing the lines.

How neatly stacked the odds are against any poet writing a distinguished libretto. The text must satisfy the various and sometimes conflicting demands of the composer, singer, and audience. It must clearly present a compelling narrative while also constantly providing intensely lyrical situations of contrasting emotion. The words must be poetic but not so rich as to block the composer's own inspiration. They must be concise but also unfold the drama in all its psychological and narrative depth. Is it any wonder that most libretti never rise above the serviceable?

VII.

Nina:	*Your play's hard to act, there are no living people in it.*
Treplev:	*Living people! We should show life neither as it is nor as it ought to be, but as we see it in our dreams.*

—Anton Chekhov, *The Seagull* (1896)

Why did I choose to write an opera libretto? It certainly was not for lack of anything else to do. I was already ridiculously overcommitted when Alva Henderson approached me. The attraction was also not financial since Henderson did not have a commission for the new project. Literary reputation played little part in my decision. Most of my fellow poets have no interest in contemporary classical music, and the libretto commands little prestige in the literary world. My interest in Henderson's proposal, however, was immediate and genuine, though my motives were not rational but intuitive and emotional. Once the composer had mentioned the project, an opera libretto seemed exactly what I wanted—and indeed *needed*—to do. Paradoxically, writing a libretto felt all the more appealing because the form was so neglected. I was also perhaps a little stage-struck. I had just finished two theatrical ventures—a full-length dance theater piece based on my poem, "Counting the Children," and a production of my translation of Seneca's Roman tragedy, *The Madness of Hercules*. Seeing those pieces performed, I had been excited by the possibilities of poetic theater. How many interesting things one might do with poetry, music, and drama under the right circumstances.

What intrigued me most specifically about working on an opera was the chance to explore the possibilities of verse drama. Could a contemporary writer create a compelling story with credible characters in the heightened language of poetry? This Shakespearean ambition has been the downfall of numerous modern poets. (Delmore Schwartz, Archibald MacLeish, Edna St. Vincent Millay, Richard Eberhart, and E. E. Cummings are five names that come immediately to mind.) Ever since the Romantic era, when poetry began to focus increasingly on inner psychological reality, verse drama has had little theatrical success. The poetic tragedies of Keats, Byron, and Shelley—not to mention those of Longfellow, Tennyson, Arnold, and Swinburne—are famous examples of Romanticism's inability to master drama. But I've always liked some of those supposedly failed lyric plays like *Prometheus Unbound* and *Manfred*. And in the Modern period I love the verse drama of Yeats, Eliot, Jeffers, and Auden. *Purgatory, Murder in the Cathedral, Medea*, and *The Ascent of F6* never fail to captivate me. (I even adore Christopher Fry's forgotten comedy, *Venus Observed*, originally written for Laurence Olivier.) Each play displays some aspect of its author's imagination not evident in the poetry. New forms open up new avenues for expression.

I had wondered, however, if words alone could still suffice for poetic drama? Back in high school I had bought an LP of Yeats's *The Only Jealousy of Emer* with background music by Lou Harrison. The simple but bewitching score intensified the dreamlike drama. How right Yeats had been to insist on the ritual elements of music, mime, and movement to support the poetry in his *Plays for Dancers*. "I have invented a form of drama, distinguished, indirect, and symbolic," he rightly boasted. W. H. Auden and Christopher Isherwood had Benjamin Britten write songs and incidental music for *Ascent of F6* and *On the Frontier*. Music and dance heighten an audience's receptivity to poetry. I saw this phenomenon vividly illustrated when the Mark Ruhala Performance Group created its dance work, *Counting the Children.* The choreography, music, and theatrical spectacle made my long and complex poem, which was spoken in its entirety by the lead dancer, overwhelmingly immediate to the audience—who were mostly not people who generally read poetry. The verse was perfectly supported and amplified by the other elements. For me, the primary appeal of opera lay in its ritual elements. Music allows the audience to experience the words not intellectually but physically, emotionally, and indeed unconsciously. Under such conditions I could explore very different ways of writing than I might use on the page.

Another impulse that led me to opera was the excitement of collaboration. Working with other artists is not always easy. The pleasure is often mixed with anxiety and frustration. But collaboration heightens one's sense of involvement. Poetry is a lonely art. I often take a single poem through fifty drafts over several years before I ever show it to someone, and even then I may choose never to publish it. But writing a libretto required me to finish every song and scene—although not always on time and rarely in the order they appear on the stage. I was keenly aware that every syllable I wrote would be studied and weighed by the composer. Then every line in the final score would be sung by a real human being who would have to become the imaginary character suggested by the words. These were not demands a poet usually faces, but I found them invigorating. I also resolved to write poetry that would be equally interesting on the page and on the stage—though perhaps in different ways.

I would not have agreed to write a libretto, however, had I not loved the music of the composer, Alva Henderson. Real collaboration requires mutual esteem—otherwise who can do their best? When I first heard Henderson's one-act opera, *The Last Leaf,* in New York in 1979, I recognized him as a rare, indeed almost unique talent. He wrote with brilliant expressivity for the voice. He also had a natural sense of theater. His characters felt genuinely alive. And he composed extraordinarily moving and memorable melodies, which embodied the dramatic action. After hearing the music from his *Medea* (1972) which uses Robinson Jeffers's powerful version, *The Last of the Mohicans* (1976) with its libretto by Janet Lewis, and many of his songs, I knew Henderson was one of America's finest vocal composers. We were close enough in style and vision to make collaboration possible but sufficiently different in temperament to make partnership interesting.

I had one unusual demand for Henderson. I asked to choose the subject of the opera. He could veto my suggestions, but I needed a story and an imaginative world that I could inhabit for the years it took to complete the project. I have gone to the opera regularly since high school—and I always go to see new or modern works. I have, however, frequently been struck by the soulless quality of many new commissions (like André Previn's *A Streetcar Named Desire* or Philip Glass's *The Voyage*) where the composer or impresario dictated some subject for which the librettist had no deep affinity. The resulting libretti are usually professionally executed but imaginatively stillborn. If you believe that a good text inspires better music—and I do—then there needs to be some genuine poetic spark of inspiration to ignite the project.

I wrote *Nosferatu* in an odd way that—to my surprise—exactly mirrored Alva's compositional approach. I would begin each scene or half-scene by writing the central aria first. (The total action of the scene had, of course, been previously plotted in a prose summary.) I wanted to create the emotional high point of the scene as a lyric poem that had some independent imaginative energy. If opera is lyric drama, then it must have lyric power. Only after finishing the aria would I write the scene that led up to and away from that moment. As it turned out, Alva liked to work this way, too—composing the major themes first and then expanding and developing them across the scene.

I happened upon the subject of *Nosferatu* by accident. I had lunch one day with the film critic, Gilberto Perez. I asked him what he was working on, and he showed me a new essay on F. W. Murnau's film. I learned from Gil, however, that I had never seen the director's original version, only a version severely cut for export. Gil gave me his essay, "The Deadly Space Between," and loaned me a videotape of the full *Nosferatu*. Reading his essay and watching the complete film, I was struck by how much Murnau's Expressionist tale of horror resembled a *bel canto* tragic opera. Surely the director had thought of his film in musical terms; he subtitled *Nosferatu* "A Symphony in Grays," and wrote the screenplay-scenario in verse. Although Murnau borrowed most of his plot from Bram Stoker's *Dracula* (which he could not legally obtain the rights to film), he simplified the story in ways that made it dramatically stronger and more resonantly symbolic. *Nosferatu* offered a librettist the positive virtues of a compelling plot, strong characters, and vivid, indeed often unforgettable, images. The silent film also afforded the negative virtues of having neither spoken words nor music. How astonishing that the Dracula legend, one of the great Romantic myths, had never served as the subject of an enduring opera. (Marschner's rarely performed 1828 opera, *Der Vampyr,* is hardly about vampirism in the modern sense of the word.) Murnau's *Nosferatu* provided a resonant but compressed version of the Dracula myth in a dramatization that left room for poetry and music.

As a child, I loved horror movies, which I knew mostly from television. On weekends my cousins and I would gather to watch the local station broadcast the black-and-white Universal films of the early talkie era—*Dracula* (1931), *Frankenstein* (1931), *The Wolfman* (1941), *The Mummy* (1932), and our collective favorite, *The Bride of Frankenstein* (1935). Such old films must have been inexpensive to broadcast because they were constantly replayed, and in those pre-videocassette days, we watched every time—often mouthing the dialogue along with Bela Lugosi or Boris Karloff. Always obsessive about my passions, I read all the movie books in the library and bought—to my parents' horror— each new issue of *Famous Monsters of Filmland.* These sources soon led me to German silent horror and fantasy films like Fritz Lang's *Metropolis* (1926) and Murnau's *Nosferatu* (1922), both of which I managed to see at age twelve. (Los Angeles offers advantages to juvenile film buffs.) *Nosferatu,* therefore, was a part of my working-class, Latin-Catholic childhood and not my university years, and I first watched it as a horror movie and not a classic of German Expressionist cinema. Perhaps for that reason working on the libretto touched other childhood memories of religion, family, and poverty. Memories of my beautiful Aunt Felice dying of cancer, the *Salve Regina* being recited at the end of our parochial school's daily morning Mass, and the constant family worries about money intermingled naturally with my first sighting of Max Schreck's shadow climbing the stairway toward his shuddering victim. I had never written about any of these early experiences before. But the new form invited new subjects, and I could disguise my life as part of someone else's story since the underlying myth was big enough to hold it all.

To write an opera libretto that might also succeed as poetic drama is to bet against the odds. Worse yet, it is to take long odds for almost no reward. But what poet today does not implicitly hazard a similar bet as a precondition of the art? Just to write a poem is to risk overwhelming odds of failure. And if one succeeds, how few notice. Why bother to write except for the joy of hard work and fresh discovery? Robert Frost once called poetry the highest kind of enterprise, "the self-appointed task," where "hard labor comes from one's own desire and internal pressure for perfection." With a haunting myth, a great film, a fine composer, and the prospect of long hard work, what more could a poet want?

DANA GIOIA was born in Los Angeles in 1950. He received his B.A. and M.B.A. degrees from Stanford University. He also has an M.A. in Comparative Literature from Harvard University. For fifteen years Gioia worked as a business executive in New York. Since 1992 he has been a full-time writer. He has published three volumes of poetry—*Daily Horoscope* (1986), *The Gods of Winter* (1991), and *Interrogations at Noon* (2001). A noted essayist and reviewer, Gioia has published a critical volume, *Can Poetry Matter?* (1992), as well as seven anthologies of poetry, fiction, and drama. He is also the classical music critic of *San Francisco* magazine and has frequently collaborated with composers. Gioia lives in Sonoma County, California, with his wife and two sons.

The text of this book is set in Minion, a typeface design by Robert Slimbach and issued by Adobe in 1989. This book was designed by Wendy Holdman, typeset by Stanton Publication Services, Inc., and manufactured by Bang Printing on acid-free paper.

Graywolf Press is a not-for-profit, independent press. The books we publish include poetry, literary fiction, essays, and cultural criticism. We are less interested in best-sellers than in talented writers who display a freshness of voice coupled with a distinct vision. We believe these are the very qualities essential to shape a vital and diverse culture.

Thankfully, many of our readers feel the same way. They have shown this through their desire to buy books by Graywolf writers; they have told us this themselves through their e-mail notes and at author events; and they have reinforced their commitment by contributing financial support, in small amounts and in large amounts, and joining the "Friends of Graywolf."

If you enjoyed this book and wish to learn more about Graywolf Press, we invite you to ask your bookseller or librarian about further Graywolf titles; or to contact us for a free catalog; or to visit our award-winning web site that features information about our forthcoming books.

We would also like to invite you to consider joining the hundreds of individuals who are already "Friends of Graywolf" by contributing to our membership program. Individual donations of any size are significant to us: they tell us that you believe that the kind of publishing we do *matters*. Our web site gives you many more details about the benefits you will enjoy as a "Friend of Graywolf"; but if you do not have online access, we urge you to contact us for a copy of our membership brochure.

www.graywolfpress.org

Graywolf Press
2402 University Avenue, Suite 203
Saint Paul, MN 55114
Phone: (651) 641-0077
Fax: (651) 641-0036
E-mail: wolves@graywolfpress.org